Cookbook
and
Party Ideas

Leslie Crouch

HYPERION
New York

Library of Congress Cataloging-in-Publication Data

Crouch, Leslie
    It's Bunco time! : cookbook and party ideas / Leslie Crouch.—1st ed.
      p. cm.
    ISBN: 1-4013-0768-X
    1. Entertaining. 2. Cookery. 3. Dice games. I. Title.

 TX731.C737 2004
 642'.4—dc22   2003067796

Hyperion books are available for special promotions and premiums. For details contact Michael Rentas, Manager, Inventory and Premium Sales, Hyperion, 77 West 66th Street, 11th floor, New York, New York 10023-6298, or call 212-456-0133.

FIRST EDITION

10   9   8   7   6   5   4   3   2   1

Contents

Introduction

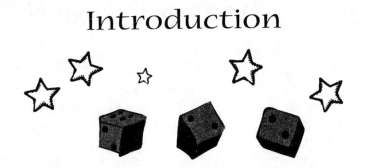

This cookbook was written to assist Bunco® players around the world with their Bunco-playing activities. We have tried to include a wide range of recipes to make your Bunco party fun, entertaining and delicious with varied recipes and themes to accommodate any type of party. We suggest using this cookbook as an integral part of every Bunco group, passing it from hostess to hostess each month. It's fun to record Bunco memories using the Bunco Night Journal entries—included throughout the cookbook in the margins and in the back of the book. Make notes about the recipes tried or directions for increasing the serving sizes for future hostesses. Don't be shy about writing on the pages—the cookbook will become a history for your Bunco group, giving new players a taste of the past.

Leslie Crouch, a mother of three and president of the World Bunco Association™, along with associates spent hours upon hours researching their data files for the best recipes and theme party ideas sent to them by subscribers of Bunco® News, as well as game players across the country and around the world through the worldbunco.com website.

Thank you to the many friends and family members who made this endeavor possible. A special thanks to Denise Riches. We appreciate all the assistance, and a special thank you goes to all the Bunco players who have supported us through the long-awaited printing of this book. This is the first edition of **It's BUNCO Time!®: Cookbook and Party Ideas,** and we hope you enjoy it. We look forward to your feedback.

Happy Bunco Playing!
The World Bunco Association™

Abbreviations/Definitions in this Cookbook

bch = bunch
btl = bottle
bx = box
c = cup
ctn = carton
gal = gallon
lb = pound
lg = large
Oleo = shortening
oz = ounces

pkg = package
pt = pint
qt = quart
scant = a little less
  than
sq = square
stk = stick
T = tablespoon
tsp = teaspoon

Many of the recipes in this book yield a smaller number of servings than you may need for your Bunco party. You will need to increase the recipe size based on your number of Bunco players. When increasing a recipe for a crowd, allow more time for preparation, chilling and cooking. But remember, don't automatically increase the seasoning ... it could overdo it. Taste and adjust as you go. If you pass this cookbook around your Bunco group, it might be helpful to note in the margins what adjustments you made to double or triple the recipes you used.

Hints & Tips

**Useful Kitchen
Information
at Your Fingertips**

Hints & Tips

Food Safety Tips

Hands and work surfaces should be cleaned with hot soapy water before and during food preparation. Use paper towels for drying hands and surfaces.

Keep raw meat, poultry and seafood away from cooked foods, as well as fresh vegetables and fruit.

Refrigerate or freeze any perishables or leftovers within 30 minutes of purchasing or within 2 hours of cooking.

Keep eggs refrigerated before cooking. Eggs should be cooked until firm, not runny.

Cooking Temperatures for Doneness

Poultry = 180 degrees
Beef, lamb, pork = 160 degrees
Ground meat and poultry = 165 degrees
Leftovers = 165 degrees (stir to reheat evenly)

Oven Temperatures

Slow oven = 250 to 325 degrees
Moderate oven = 350 to 375 degrees
Hot oven = 400 to 450 degrees
Very hot oven = 450 to 500 degrees

Baking Substitutions

Save a last-minute trip to the grocery store with these baking alternatives.

1 teaspoon double-acting baking powder = ¼ teaspoon baking soda plus ½ teaspoon cream of tartar.

1 cup butter = 1 cup margarine or solid shortening, or ⅞ cup lard.

1 cup buttermilk = 1 tablespoon lemon juice or white vinegar plus enough milk to make 1 cup (let sit 5 minutes), or 1 cup unflavored yogurt.

1 cup unsifted cake flour = 1 cup unsifted all-purpose flour minus 2 table-spoons (minus ¼ cup, total, if recipe calls for sifted cake flour).

1 cup milk = ½ cup canned evaporated milk plus ½ cup water, or ⅓ cup instant nonfat dried milk stirred into 1 cup water.

1 cup unsifted self-rising flour = 1 cup unsifted all-purpose flour, 1½ tea-spoons baking powder, and ¼ teaspoon salt.

1 cup sour cream = 1 cup unflavored yogurt.

1 ounce unsweetened chocolate = 3 tablespoons unsweetened cocoa plus 1 tablespoon melted butter, margarine, or shortening.

1 cup whipping cream = ¾ cup milk plus ⅓ cup melted butter or margarine. Use for baking, not whipping.

Simplified Measures

Dash = 2 or 3 drops, or
less than ⅛ teaspoon
3 teaspoons = 1 tablespoon
1 tablespoon = 3 teaspoons
2 tablespoons = ⅛ cup
4 tablespoons = ¼ cup
8 tablespoons = ½ cup
12 tablespoons = ¾ cup
16 tablespoons = 1 cup
¼ cup = 4 tablespoons
⅓ cup = 5 tablespoons plus
1 teaspoon

½ cup = 8 tablespoons
1 pint = 2 cups
2 pints = 1 quart
1 quart = 4 cups
1 gallon = 4 quarts
1 peck = 8 quarts
1 bushel = 8 pecks
4 ounces = ½ cup
8 ounces = 1 cup
16 ounces = 1 pound

Equivalents

Apples, 1 pound = 3 medium or 3 cups sliced
Bananas, 3 medium = 1 cup mashed
Berries, 1 pint = 1¾ cups
Bread, 1-pound loaf = 14–20 slices
Butter or margarine, 1 pound = 2 cups or 4 sticks
Cheese, ¼ pound = 1 cup shredded
Cheese, 1 pound = 4 cups shredded
Cheese, cottage, 8 ounces = 1 cup
Cheese, cream, 3 ounces = 6 tablespoons

Chocolate, unsweetened, 8 ounces = 8 squares
Crackers, graham, 14 squares = 1 cup crumbs
Crackers, saltines, 28 = 1 cup crumbs
Cream, heavy or whipping, 1 cup = 2 cups whipped cream
Garlic, 1 small clove pressed = 1/8 teaspoon dry
Lemon, 1 medium = 3 tablespoons juice; 2 tablespoons grated peel
Onion, 1 medium = 3/4 to 1 cup chopped
Onion, 1 small = 1 tablespoon instant minced onion
Macaroni, 4 ounces uncooked (1 to 1¼ cups) = 2¼ cups cooked
Marshmallows, 10 miniature = 1 large
Noodles, 4 ounces uncooked (1½ to 2 cups) = 2 cups cooked
Orange, 1 medium = 1/3 to 1/2 cup juice; 2 tablespoons grated peel
Potatoes, 1 pound = 3 medium
Sugar, 1 pound brown = 2¼ cups
Sugar, 1 pound powdered = 2½ cups packed

Metric Conversion Charts

Tablespoons and Ounces	Grams
1 pinch = less than 1/3 teaspoon (dry)	0.5 grams
1 dash = 3 drops to 1/4 teaspoon (liquid)	1.25 grams
1 teaspoon (liquid)	5.0 grams
3 teaspoons = 1 tablespoon = 1/2 ounce	14.3 grams
2 tablespoons = 1 ounce	28.35 grams
4 tablespoons = 2 ounces = 1/4 cup	56.7 grams
8 tablespoons = 4 ounces = 1/2 cup (1 stick of butter)	113.4 grams
8 tablespoons (flour) = about 2 ounces	72.0 grams
16 tablespoons = 8 ounces = 1 cup	226.8 grams
32 tablespoons = 16 ounces = 2 cups	453.6 grams or 0.4536 kilograms
64 tablespoons = 32 ounces = 1 quart	907 grams or 0.907 kilograms
1 quart	roughly 1 liter

Spices and Herbs

Allspice—Resembles a blend of cloves, cinnamon and nutmeg. Use in meat, poultry, pickles, relishes, cakes, cookies and pastry.

Anise seed—Aroma and flavor resemble licorice. Use with fruits and in breads, cookies, candies and other desserts.

Basil—Faintly anise-like flavor. Use with tomatoes, peas, squash, lamb, fish, eggs, salads and potatoes.

Bay leaves—Pungent flavor. Use with vegetables and soups; in tomato sauce dishes; pot roast and stews; pickles and fish.

Caraway—Flavor that combines the tastes of anise and dill. Use for baking breads; often added to sauerkraut, noodles, cheese spreads. Also adds zest to French fried potatoes.

Cumin—Strong flavor and aroma. Use in Spanish, Mexican and some Italian meat and rice dishes; with cheese spreads. Use a light hand . . . a little goes a long way!

Curry—Distinctive flavor and golden color. Characteristic flavor of Indian cuisine. Use in meat, poultry, egg and cheese dishes; in sauces, salad dressings and soups. Use a light hand.

Dill—Flavor and aroma slightly sharp. Used in pickles; to flavor cheese dishes, salad dressings, dips and with vegetables. Use as a garnish.

Marjoram—Has a minty-sweet flavor. Use in beverages, jellies and to flavor soups, stews, fish and sauces.

Mint—Flavor and aroma strong and sweet. Use with vegetables, fruits, desserts; in jelly, tea, relishes and also as a garnish.

Oregano—Flavor and aroma similar to marjoram and thyme but stronger. Often used in Italian- and Mexican-style main courses and sauces.

Paprika—Distinctive red color. Flavor and aroma slightly sweet with a bite. Use in meat, poultry and cheese dishes; also in sauces, dips, dressings and as a garnish.

Parsley—Flavor and aroma mild, characteristic in soup, salads, meat, poultry, seafood, cheese, egg and vegetable dishes. Use as a garnish. Rich in minerals.

Poppy—Has a rich fragrance and crunchy, nut-like flavor. Excellent as a topping for breads, rolls and cookies.

Rosemary—A sweet, fresh taste. Use in lamb dishes, soups and stews.

Sage—Aroma slightly bitter. Enhances flavor of meat, poultry, cheese, eggs and stuffing dishes.

Thyme—A strong, distinctive flavor. Use for poultry seasoning in croquettes, fricassees and fish dishes. Also tasty on fresh-sliced tomatoes.

Turmeric—A mild, ginger-pepper flavor. Use as a flavoring and coloring in prepared mustard and in combination with mustard as a flavoring for meats, dressings and salads.

Miscellaneous Household Tips

Let raw potatoes stand in ice-cold water for at least 30 minutes before frying to improve crispness.

To make smooth gravy or sauces, use your electric blender or keep a paste made of ⅓ cup flour mixed with ⅔ cup water. Pour into pan drippings as needed for gravy or sauce.

Don't boil a sauce that contains more than half milk. The secret is to simmer . . . the pot will be easier to clean too.

Add a tablespoon of sour cream to gravies and sauces for extra flavor. Great in mashed or whipped potatoes.

Stuff a miniature marshmallow in the bottom of a sugar cone to prevent ice cream drips.

Use a meat baster to "squeeze" your pancake batter onto the hot griddle—perfectly shaped pancakes every time.

To keep potatoes from budding, place an apple in the bag with the potatoes.

To keep marshmallow from sticking to your fingers when making Rice Krispie treats, run your hands under cold water before pressing them into the pan.

To easily remove burnt-on food from your skillet, simply add a drop or two of dish soap and enough water to cover bottom of pan, and bring to a boil on stove-top; skillet will be much easier to clean now.

Spray your Tupperware with nonstick cooking spray before pouring in tomato-based sauces; no more stains.

When a cake recipe calls for flouring the baking pan, use a bit of the dry cake mix instead—no white mess on the outside of the cake.

If you accidentally oversalt a dish while it's still cooking, drop in a peeled potato—it absorbs the excess salt for an instant "fix me up."

Wrap celery in aluminum foil before putting in the refrigerator—it will keep for weeks.

Brush beaten egg white over pie crust before baking to yield a beautiful glossy finish.

Place a slice of apple in hardened brown sugar to soften it back up.

When boiling corn on the cob, add a pinch of sugar to help bring out the corn's natural sweetness.

To determine whether an egg is fresh, immerse it in a pan of cool, salted water. If it sinks, it is fresh—if it rises to the surface, throw it away.

Cure for headaches: Take a lime, cut it in half and rub it on your forehead. The throbbing will go away.

If you have a problem opening jars: Try using latex dishwashing gloves. They give a nonslip grip that makes opening jars easy.

Potatoes will take food stains off your fingers. Just slice and rub raw potato on the stains and rinse with water.

To get rid of the itch from mosquito bites: Try applying soap on the area, instant relief.

Ants, ants, ants everywhere . . . Well, they are said to never cross a chalk line. So get your chalk out and draw a line on the floor or wherever ants tend to march—see for yourself.

Use air freshener to clean mirrors: It does a good job and, better still, leaves a lovely smell to the shine.

When you get a splinter, reach for the Scotch tape before resorting to tweezers or a needle. Simply put the Scotch tape over the splinter, then pull it off. Tape removes most splinters painlessly and easily.

Look what you can do with Alka-Seltzer:

- Clean a toilet—drop in two Alka-Seltzer tablets, wait twenty minutes, brush and flush.
- The citric acid and effervescent action clean vitreous china.
- Clean a vase—to remove a stain from the bottom of a glass vase or cruet, fill with water and drop in two Alka-Seltzer tablets.
- Polish jewelry—drop two Alka-Seltzer tablets into a glass of water and immerse the jewelry for two minutes.
- Clean a thermos bottle—fill the bottle with water, drop in four Alka-Seltzer tablets, and let soak for an hour (or longer, if necessary).
- Unclog a drain—clear the sink drain by dropping three Alka-Seltzer tablets down the drain followed by a cup of Heinz White Vinegar. Wait a few minutes, then run the hot water.

Your Own Hints & Tips

Great Bunco Beginnings

**Easy and Delicious
Beverages and Appetizers
for a Fabulous
Party Warm-up**

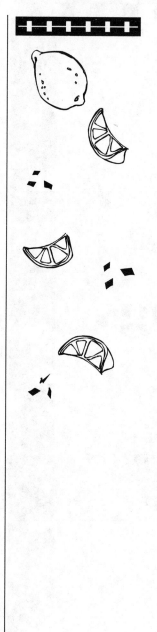

Beverages

Real Old-Fashioned Lemonade

1 c	fresh-squeezed lemon juice
3/4 c	sugar
4 c	cold water
1	lemon, sliced in cartwheel slices
	ice cubes

In a large pitcher, combine lemon juice and sugar. Stir to dissolve sugar. Add remaining ingredients and blend well. Yield: six 8-ounce servings.

Chris Smyth, Charlotte, North Carolina

Creamy Punch

1/2 gal	vanilla ice cream
4 c	orange juice
1/2 c	lemon juice
2 btls	lemon-lime carbonated beverage (28 oz), chilled

Spoon ice cream into punch bowl. Add the orange and lemon juice. Stir. Slowly add the lemon-lime carbonated beverage. Stir gently, punch will be very foamy. Ladle into punch cups.

Dorothy Dahms, Newport Beach, California

Eggnog

4	eggs
1/2 c	sugar
1/4 tsp	salt
4 c	milk
1 tsp	vanilla
	nutmeg to taste

Combine all ingredients in a blender. Blend, pour into glasses. Add a pinch of nutmeg if desired.

Sue Miller, Costa Mesa, California

Mint Julep

What a treat to be served—a frosty glass of mint julep as a special beginning to a warm summer evening Bunco party.

17	lemons
3½ c	sugar
3 c	water
32	sprigs of mint
	ice cubes
6–8 c	sour mash bourbon
	juice of 16 of the lemons, reserving the rinds

In a small heavy saucepan, dissolve 3 cups of the sugar into the water, then add the lemon rinds and cook over medium heat until the liquid becomes syrupy, approximately 15 minutes. Cool to room temperature. Place the remaining ½ cup sugar on a small plate. Cut the remaining lemon into quarters. Rub the wedges along the rims of 12 tall glasses and invert the glasses in the sugar to create a sugar rim. Crush a mint sprig into the bottom of each glass with a wooden reamer. Fill each glass with ice cubes and divide the lemon juice and syrup equally among the glasses. Top off with about ½ cup of bourbon per glass. Garnish each glass with a fresh sprig of mint. There might even be a little extra left over for those extra-thirsty mint julep drinkers.

Missy Frank, Carlsbad, California

Citrus Squeezing

To get the most juice out of fresh lemons, oranges, or limes, bring them to room temperature and roll them under your palm against the kitchen counter before squeezing.

Mai Tai Cocktail

A nice refreshing starter to any Bunco night.

	finely crushed ice or shaved ice
2 T	light rum
¼ c	mai tai mix (or you may use several of your own favorite fruit juices combined for the mix, if desired)
6 T	freshly squeezed orange juice
	lime for garnish

Fill a double old-fashioned glass with ice, add the rum, mai tai mix and orange juice, and mix well. Garnish with lime slice. Yield: 1 drink.

Connie Withers, Encinitas, California

Margarita

	lime wedges
	coarse kosher salt
	ice cubes
1¼ c	freshly squeezed lime juice
1 c	best quality white tequila
⅓ c	Cointreau
⅓ c	sugar (or more to taste)

To salt-rim the stemmed glasses, rub cut lime around the rim. Fill a saucer with salt and dip the goblet, upside down, into the salt. Refrigerate goblets until ready to use. Fill a blender three-quarters full of ice cubes. Pour lime juice, tequila and Cointreau over the ice. Add the sugar and blend, starting slowly and then setting the blender at high speed, until the ice is very finely chopped and the mixture is frothy. Taste for sweetness, adding more sugar if necessary. Blend a few minutes more and pour into chilled glasses. Serve immediately. Yield: 4 large drinks.

Bonnie Andrews, Austin, Texas

Tennessee Iced Tea

A fresh-tasting punch like this is even better when a wonderful fruit-flavored tea is used.

	chipped ice
1 qt	freshly squeezed orange juice
1 qt	fresh-brewed tea, cooled
2 T	honey
¾ c	golden rum, such as Mount Gay
1	orange, thinly sliced crosswise and quartered

Fill a large pitcher with ice and stir in the orange juice, tea, honey and rum (you may need to use two pitchers). Serve over ice in tall glasses and garnish with orange slices.

Helen Curtis, Indianapolis, Indiana

Ocean Sunrise

	juice of one lime
3 T	cranberry juice
3 T	tequila
	crushed ice

Put all ingredients in a cocktail shaker; shake well. Yield: 1 generous drink.

Lois Grand, Louisville, Kentucky

Kiwi Cooler

2–3 c	crushed ice
¾ c	vodka
2 T	coconut cream
	kiwi fruit, peeled and sliced
	juice of 2 lemons
	kiwi fruit slices for garnish

In a blender, blend all ingredients (except garnish) until frothy. Serve in chilled glasses, garnished with kiwi fruit slices. Yield: 4 drinks.

Sandra Porter, Boston, Massachusetts

Bunco Night JOURNAL

Date of Party
_____

Hostess
_____

Party Theme
_____

Menu
_____
_____
_____
_____

Winners
_____
_____
_____
_____
_____

Who Else Played
_____
_____
_____
_____
_____
_____

Memories of the Evening
_____
_____
_____
_____

Mulled Wine

A great holiday warmer.

4 btls	Burgundy wine
1 tsp	allspice berries
1	cinnamon stick, 2-inch
12	whole cloves
½ c	sugar
½ tsp	Angostura bitters

*C*ombine all ingredients and heat, but do not boil. Let sit, hot, until ready to serve. Strain into a heated punch bowl or Crock-Pot and serve. Yield: about 32 drinks.

Anna Feldman, Beverly Hills, California

Waste Not!

Don't throw out all that leftover wine: Freeze into ice cubes for future use in casseroles and sauces.

Dips and Spreads

Clam Dip

1 pkg	cream cheese (8 oz)
1 can	minced clams
1 T	clam juice
3 tsp	Worcestershire sauce
1	large clove garlic, minced
	salt

*C*ut cream cheese into chunks; add to small saucepan. Add remaining ingredients to pan. Cook over medium heat until just bubbly. Serve immediately with potato chips or crackers.

Vera Riches, Thousand Oaks, California

Salsa

Adjust the hotness of this no-cook salsa to your liking by adding some jalapeño peppers or bottled hot pepper sauce.

2 cans	diced tomatoes (14½ oz each)
1 can	diced green chili peppers (4 oz)
¼ c	green onions, thinly sliced
¼ c	snipped cilantro or parsley
2 T	lemon juice
⅛ tsp	pepper
1	clove garlic, minced
1	recipe Tortilla Crisps (page 28)

Sandra Porter, Boston, Massachusetts

Warm Cheddar Dip

¼ c	milk
¼ lb	cream cheese
1 c	Cheddar cheese, shredded
½ tsp	dry mustard
½ tsp	Worcestershire sauce
	dash hot pepper sauce
3	green onions, chopped

In a saucepan, combine milk and cream cheese over low heat. Using a whisk, blend until smooth. Increase heat to medium and stir in Cheddar cheese until melted. Stir in mustard, Worcestershire, hot pepper sauce and half the green onions. Cook until heated through; pour into serving dish. Top with remaining green onions.

Tina Farley, Yuma, Arizona

Spinach Dip

1 pkg	uncooked spinach, chopped and drained
1 can	water chestnuts
1 pkg	Knorr's Leek Soup or vegetable soup
1 c	sour cream
1 c	mayonnaise

1   round loaf of bread, center of loaf torn into bite-size pieces, reserving shell to serve dip in

Mix well. Serve with torn-up bread pieces for dipping.

Donna Thomas, Fremont, California

Chunky Chicken Spread/Dip

1 can   chunky chicken spread (4¼ oz)
1 pkg   cream cheese (8 oz)
¼ tsp   soy sauce
¼ tsp   sesame oil

Mix well and refrigerate. Serve with sesame crackers.

Vera Riches, Thousand Oaks, California

Artichoke Dip

2 jars   marinated artichokes (6 oz each)
1 c   mayonnaise
2 c   cheese, Parmesan, mozzarella, Jack

Mix together. Heat in a 350° oven for 30 minutes or until bubbly.

Beth Elster, Irvine, California

Mexican Eight-Layer Dip

2–3 c   shredded lettuce
1 can   bean dip (9 oz)
¼ c   picante or taco sauce
1 ctn   sour cream (8 oz)
1 ctn   frozen avocado dip (6 oz), thawed
1 c   shredded Cheddar or Jack cheese (4 oz)
¼ c   sliced green onions
2 T   pitted ripe olives, sliced or chopped
⅔ c   tomato, chopped and seeded
        tortilla chips or crackers

*O*n a platter, arrange lettuce, leaving a 2-inch open rim at edge of platter. Combine bean dip and picante sauce. Spread bean mixture over lettuce, making a layer ¼-inch thick. Next, layer sour cream and avocado dip. Top with cheese, onions, and olives. Cover and chill 4 to 24 hours. Before serving, sprinkle with chopped tomato. Arrange the chips or crackers on the platter around spread. Yield: 16 appetizer servings.

Sandra White, Santa Fe, New Mexico

Cowboy Caviar

1 can	black-eyed peas (15 oz), rinsed and drained
¼ c	green onions, thinly sliced
¼ c	red sweet pepper, finely chopped
2	cloves garlic, minced
2 T	cooking oil
2 T	cider vinegar
1–2	fresh jalapeño peppers, seeded and chopped
¼ tsp	cracked black pepper
	dash salt
	assorted crackers or tortilla chips

*I*n a bowl, combine black-eyed peas, green onions, sweet pepper, garlic, oil, vinegar, jalapeño peppers, black pepper and salt. Cover and chill overnight. To serve, transfer to a serving dish. Serve with crackers or tortilla chips. Cover any leftovers; chill for up to 4 days. Yield: 2 cups.

Mickie Paulins, Fort Worth, Texas

Chili Con Queso

½ c	onion, finely chopped
1 T	margarine or butter
1⅓ c	tomatoes, chopped and seeded
1 can	diced green chili peppers (4 oz), drained
1 c	American cheese, shredded
1 c	Monterey Jack cheese, shredded

Bunco Night JOURNAL

Date of Party

Hostess

Party Theme

Menu

Winners

Who Else Played

Memories of the Evening

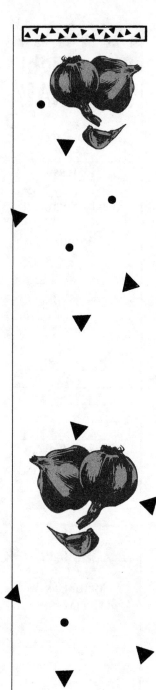

In a saucepan, cook onion in margarine or butter till tender. Stir in tomatoes and chili peppers. Simmer uncovered for 10 minutes. Toss cheeses with cornstarch. Gradually add cheese mixture to saucepan, stirring till melted. Stir in hot pepper sauce; heat through. Serve with chips. Yield: 1¾ cups.

Janet Yearling, Little Rock, Arkansas

3-2-1 Dip

1½ c	Cheddar cheese, shredded
1½ c	Swiss cheese, shredded
2 c	mayonnaise
1 c	onions, chopped
¼ c	diced chilies

Mix together and bake at 350° for 20 minutes. Serve with chips, vegetables or other munchies.

Darlene Davenport, Bangor, Maine

Guacamole

1½	avocados, mashed
3	green onions, chopped
1	tomato, chopped
2	jalapeño peppers, finely chopped
	cilantro to taste
	salt and pepper
	juice from half a lemon

Mix together and serve with your favorite tortilla chips.

Marian Kinny, New Orleans, Louisiana

Chili Dip

Use one can of chili with jalapeños to add a spicy flavor.

1 can	chili with beans
1 can	chili with no beans
1 pkg	cream cheese (8 oz)

Heat chili in saucepan or small Crock-Pot. Cut up cream cheese and mix with chili. Stir well until mixed thoroughly. Serve with tortilla chips.

Jessica Cassese, Irvine, California

Cheddar Cheese Ball

1 c	Cheddar cheese, finely shredded
1 pkg	cream cheese (3 oz)
2 T	margarine or butter
1 T	milk or dry white wine
1 T	green onion, finely chopped
1 T	diced pimiento
1 tsp	Worcestershire sauce
	dash bottled hot pepper sauce
1/3 c	snipped parsley or finely chopped walnuts or pecans
	assorted crackers

Bring the cheeses and margarine to room temperature. Add milk, green onions, pimiento, Worcestershire sauce and hot pepper sauce; beat until combined. Cover and chill 4 to 24 hours. Shape mixture into a ball; roll in parsley or nuts. Let stand 15 minutes. Serve with crackers. Yield: 1½ cups.

Blue Cheese Ball: Prepare as above, except omit pimiento, add ¼ cup crumbled "blue cheese" (1 oz) to cheese mixture, and substitute chopped, toasted almonds for the parsley or nuts.

Jennifer Thomas, Honolulu, Hawaii

Bunco Night JOURNAL

Date of Party
_____

Hostess
_____

Party Theme
_____

Menu
_____
_____
_____
_____

Winners
_____
_____
_____
_____
_____

Who Else Played
_____
_____
_____
_____
_____

Memories
of the Evening
_____
_____
_____
_____

Appetizers and Snacks

Acapulco Shrimp Cocktail

1 lb	medium raw shrimp (16–20)
1/3 c	white onion, minced
1/2 c	cucumber, peeled, seeded and finely diced
1 lg	tomato, peeled, seeded and cut into 1/4-inch diced pieces
1	jalapeño pepper, seeded and minced
1/4 c	chopped cilantro
1/3 c	ketchup
	juice of 2 limes
1/4 tsp	salt
1 lg	ripe avocado cut into 1/2-inch pieces (optional)

In a medium saucepan of boiling water, cook shrimp until pink and loosely curled, 2 to 3 minutes. Drain and rinse under cold running water to cool. Shell and devein shrimp. Place in a medium bowl, cover, and refrigerate about 1 hour, or until cold. In another medium bowl, combine onion, cucumber, tomato, jalapeño pepper, cilantro, ketchup, lime juice and salt. Gently mix in avocado and cold shrimp. Divide among 6 cocktail glasses. Serve at once as a first course. Yield: 6 servings.

Sunny Holden, Denver, Colorado

Buffalo Wings

12	chicken wings
1/2 tsp	salt
1/8 tsp	pepper
8 T	butter
2 T	vegetable oil
1/2 c	taco sauce

½ c	barbecue sauce
¼ c	French dressing
⅛ tsp	red pepper sauce
⅛ tsp	Worcestershire sauce

Heat oven to 300°. Cut off and discard tips of each wing at first joint; cut apart the two remaining parts at the joint. Sprinkle both sides of wings with salt and pepper. Heat 2 tablespoons butter and the oil in a large skillet over medium heat. Cook half the wings in the butter mixture until golden, 8 to 10 minutes on each side. Remove wings and repeat for remaining wings. Melt remaining 6 tablespoons butter in 1-quart saucepan; blend in remaining ingredients. Arrange wings in shallow baking pan. Brush with enough taco sauce mixture to coat evenly. Bake until hot, 5 to 8 minutes. Arrange wings on serving plate. Pour remaining taco sauce mixture into bowl; serve as dip for wings.

Teresa Perris, Long Beach, California

Spinach and Cheese Squares

4 oz	butter
3	eggs
1 c	flour
1 c	milk
1 tsp	salt
1 tsp	baking powder
1 lb	Jack cheese, shredded
4 c	fresh spinach, chopped

Melt butter in a 9 × 13 inch pan. Beat eggs and add flour, milk, salt and baking powder. Add cheese and spinach, mix well. Spread into pan and bake at 350° for 35 minutes. Cool 30 minutes before serving. Cut into squares. Yield: 40 squares.

Sally Moore, Phoenix, Arizona

Pork Wontons

½ lb	ground pork
¼ tsp	salt
½ tsp	sugar
½ tsp	cornstarch
1½ tsp	butter
1 tsp	soy sauce
1 T	sherry
2	green onions, chopped
½ lb	wonton skins
1	egg white
2 c	peanut oil
1	recipe wonton sauce (below)

Cook ground pork over medium heat about five minutes. Pour off fat. Add salt, sugar, cornstarch, butter, soy sauce, sherry and green onions. Mix and refrigerate until cool. Dab each wonton skin with ½ tsp filling. Moisten edges with egg white. Fold each wonton skin into a triangle and seal edges well. Fill all wonton skins before cooking. Place on wax paper and cover with plastic wrap to prevent skins from drying out. Do not stack or let skins touch before cooking. Heat wok or skillet; add oil. When hot, cook 6 to 8 wontons at a time until golden brown; drain on paper towel and serve immediately. Dip in wonton sauce.

Wonton Sauce:

2 T	cornstarch
1 c	chicken broth
½ c	pineapple juice
3 T	ketchup
3 T	wine vinegar
4 T	sugar
½ tsp	soy sauce

Beat all ingredients together in a small saucepan. Cook, stirring constantly, until sauce thickens.

Melody Traverse, Portland, Oregon

Cheesy Artichoke Squares

4	eggs
1/2 tsp	salt
1/2 tsp	oregano
1/2 c	onion, chopped
2 T	butter
2 cans	marinated artichokes (6 oz), drained and chopped
1/4 c	bread crumbs
	dash of pepper
4 drops	hot pepper sauce
1	clove garlic, minced
2 c	Cheddar cheese, shredded

Mix first 6 ingredients in bowl. Sauté onion and garlic in the butter. Add onion mixture to bread crumb mixture. Add cheese and artichokes. Spread mixture one inch thick in baking dish and bake at 350° for 30 minutes. Cool and cut into small squares. Serve warm or at room temperature.

Madison Vickers, Encinitas, California

Stuffed Mushrooms

24 lg	fresh mushrooms, 1½ to 2 inches in diameter
1/4 c	green onions, sliced
1	clove garlic, minced
1/4 c	margarine or butter
2/3 c	fine dry bread crumbs
1/2 c	Cheddar cheese, shredded or crumbled blue cheese (2 oz.)

Rinse and drain mushrooms. Remove stems; reserve caps. Chop enough stems to make one cup. In a medium saucepan, cook the chopped stems, green onions and garlic in margarine or butter until tender. Stir in bread crumbs and cheese. Spoon crumb mixture into mushroom

**Bunco Night
JOURNAL**

Date of Party
_____

Hostess
_____

Party Theme
_____

Menu
_____
_____
_____
_____

Winners
_____
_____
_____
_____
_____

Who Else Played
_____
_____
_____
_____
_____

**Memories
of the Evening**
_____
_____
_____
_____
_____

Notes

caps. Arrange mushrooms in a 15 × 10 × 1 inch baking pan. Bake in a 450° oven for 8 to 10 minutes or until heated through. Yield: 24 mushrooms.

Mackenzie Leigh, Nashville, Tennessee

Cocktail Meatballs

½ lb	lean ground beef
¼ lb	ground pork
¼ lb	lamb
½ c	bread crumbs
½ c	sherry
1	small onion, minced
1	egg, beaten
1	clove garlic, minced
1 T	parsley flakes
½ tsp	salt
½ tsp	pepper
½ tsp	oregano
½ tsp	basil
½ tsp	thyme

Sauce:

1 c	chili sauce
½ c	apple jelly
1 tsp	paprika
1 tsp	basil

Preheat oven to 350°. Mix the ground meats together thoroughly. Blend in all remaining ingredients. Shape into small balls. Bake in oven for 12 minutes or until done. Drain on paper towel. Mix the chili sauce, jelly and seasonings together in a saucepan. Heat slowly until hot; **do not boil.**

Place meatballs in serving dish, pour sauce over meatballs and serve.

John Albert, Cleveland, Ohio

Smoked Salmon Pizza

Great one for the BBQ.

1 lb	frozen bread dough, thawed
1/3 c	olive oil
1 c	sour cream
1/4 lb	thinly sliced smoked salmon
1/4 c	red onion, chopped
1 T	fresh dill, chopped, or 1 tsp dried dill
1 T	freshly ground pepper
	lemon wedges

Prepare a low fire. Divide bread dough in half and flatten into two 6-inch rounds about 1/2-inch thick. Generously brush one side of each pizza with oil and place oiled side down on side of oiled grill. Cook, covered, until browned and firm, about 5 to 7 minutes. (If crust becomes too dark at edges, move to a cooler part of grill.) Brush tops of dough with oil and turn pizza over. Grill, moving if crust is getting too dark, 5 to 7 minutes, or until nicely browned and crisp.

Remove pizzas from grill and spread sour cream on top of each. Arrange salmon slices over sour cream and top with red onion, dill and pepper. Serve with lemon wedges.

Vicki Carter, Medford, Oregon

Chili-Baked Shrimp

Convenient oven-baked shrimp can be served hot or at room temperature for a spicy appetizer, with nuts, chips and cold beer.

1 T	New Mexico or pasilla chili powder
1/2 tsp	dried oregano
1/4 tsp	ground cumin
1/4 tsp	ground cinnamon
1/8 tsp	ground allspice
1/4 tsp	salt
2	cloves garlic, crushed

1 T fresh lime juice
1 T vegetable oil
1 lb large uncooked shrimp (16–20), shelled, deveined with tails intact

In a medium bowl, combine all ingredients except shrimp. Mix well. Add shrimp and toss to coat completely. Cover and marinate in refrigerator at least 1 hour or up to 6 hours.

Preheat oven to 500°. Remove shrimp from refrigerator and place on a lightly greased baking sheet in a single layer. Let stand at room temperature about 15 minutes before cooking. Bake 3 to 5 minutes, until shrimp are pink, curled and opaque throughout. Serve hot or at room temperature.

Michelle Bond, Casper, Wyoming

Tortilla Crisps

Make plain or cinnamon Tortilla Crisps to serve with salsa or other dips or spreads.
12 7- to 8-inch flour tortillas

Cut each tortilla into 8 wedges. Spread one-third of the wedges in a 15 × 10 × 1 inch baking pan. Bake at 350° for 5 to 10 minutes or until dry and crisp. Repeat with remaining wedges; cool. Store in an airtight container at room temperature up to 4 days or in the freezer up to 3 weeks. Yield: 96 crisps (24 appetizer servings).

Cinnamon Tortilla Crisps: Prepare as plain crisps, except combine ½ cup sugar and 1 teaspoon ground cinnamon. Brush ¼ cup melted margarine or butter over tortillas; sprinkle with cinnamon-sugar mixture. Cut each tortilla into 8 wedges.

Sue Whitney, Long Beach, California

Quesadillas

Try cooked chicken or vegetables in place of the bacon or sausage.

2 c	Colby and Monterey Jack cheese (8 oz), shredded
7	8-inch flour tortillas
3 T	canned diced green chili peppers, drained
3 T	green onions, chopped
3	bacon slices, crisp-cooked, drained, and crumbled, or ¼ pound bulk Italian sausage, cooked and drained
	salsa (optional)

Sprinkle ⅓ cup cheese over half of each tortilla. Top with chili peppers, green onions and bacon or sausage. Fold tortillas in half, press gently. In a 10-inch skillet, cook quesadillas, 2 at a time, over medium heat for 2 to 3 minutes or until lightly browned, turning once. Remove quesadillas from skillet; place on a baking sheet. Keep warm in a 300° oven. Repeat with remaining quesadillas. To serve, cut quesadillas into wedges. If desired, serve with salsa. Yield: 6 servings.

Kathleen Douglas, Memphis, Tennessee

Spicy Party Cheesecake

2 pkgs	cream cheese (8 oz), softened
2 c	Monterey Jack cheese (8 oz), shredded
2 ctns	dairy sour cream (8 oz)
3	eggs
1 c	salsa
1 can	diced green chili peppers (4 oz), drained
1 ctn	frozen avocado dip (6 oz), thawed
⅔ c	tomato, chopped and seeded
1	recipe Tortilla Crisps (page 28) or purchased tortilla chips or large corn chips
	fresh cilantro or parsley sprigs (optional)

Bunco Night JOURNAL

Date of Party

Hostess

Party Theme

Menu

Winners

Who Else Played

Memories of the Evening

eat cheeses with an electric mixer till light and fluffy. Beat in 1 carton sour cream. Add eggs all at once; beat on low speed just till combined. Stir in salsa and chili peppers. Pour into a 9-inch springform pan. Place on a baking sheet. Bake in a 350° oven 40 to 45 minutes or until center is almost set. Immediately spread remaining carton sour cream over top of cheesecake. Cool on a rack. Cover; chill 3 to 24 hours.

To serve, remove sides of pan. Spoon avocado dip around edge of cheesecake and sprinkle with tomato. Cut into wedges and serve with Tortilla Crisps. If desired, garnish with cilantro. Yield: 20 appetizer servings.

Judy Brighton, Los Angeles, California

Empanadas

½ lb	lean ground beef
¼ c	minced onion
3 T	red chili salsa, hot or mild
1 tsp	chili powder
½ tsp	ground cumin
½ tsp	garlic powder
½ tsp	ground coriander
	salt and pepper to taste
1 pkg	frozen patty shells (10 oz), thawed

o make beef filling, crumble and sauté beef and onion in a skillet until beef is cooked and onion is soft. Drain. Stir in red chili salsa, chili powder, cumin, garlic powder, coriander, salt and pepper. Set aside. Place thawed patty shell dough on a floured board and roll out all in one piece to about ¹⁄₁₆-inch thickness. Cut dough into rounds with a 3-inch round cookie cutter or a large drinking glass. Put 2 teaspoons of filling on each dough circle. Fold each over into a half-circle. Moisten edges with water and press edges together with a fork. Place empanadas slightly apart on an ungreased cookie sheet. Prick tops with a fork.

Bake at 400° for 20 minutes or until golden brown. Serve hot. These may be wrapped carefully after baking and frozen. To reheat, bake frozen empanadas uncovered at 400° for 7 to 8 minutes. Yield: 20 empanadas.

Cory West, Galveston, Texas

Ceviche

1 lb	firm, white fish filets
	juice of 12 limes
3	bay leaves
¼ tsp	white pepper
1 tsp	seasoned salt
1	clove garlic, minced
⅓ c	onion, chopped
1 tsp	crushed red pepper
1 tsp	salt
¼ c	sliced, stuffed olives
¼ c	juice from olives
1 T	vegetable oil
¼ c	ketchup
2	tomatoes, finely chopped
1	hot green chili (jalapeño), chopped

Remove tissue-like skin and cut fish into very thin strips, 1 inch long. Put fish in a glass jar and cover with lime juice. Refrigerate overnight. Drain and combine fish with remaining ingredients. Store in refrigerator for at least 1 hour. This will keep well for several days. To serve, remove bay leaves and serve in individual dishes with a garnish of lettuce or lime slice, or serve as a dip with tortilla chips. Yield: 6–8 servings.

Kelly Lawson, Osaka, Japan

Green Chili Bites

1 can	mild green chilies (4 oz), chopped
4 c	sharp Cheddar cheese, shredded (1 lb)
6	eggs, beaten

Butter the bottom of an 8 × 8 inch baking pan. Spread green chilies on bottom. Sprinkle shredded cheese over chilies, and pour eggs over all. Bake uncovered at 350° for 30 minutes, or until firm. Cut into 1-inch squares. Serve hot on a warming tray. Yield: 64 pieces.

Elaine Foster, San Mateo, California

Flavored Popcorn

6 c	warm popped popcorn (about ¼ c unpopped)
2 T	butter or margarine
2 T	Parmesan cheese, 1 T American cheese food, or 1 tsp taco seasoning mix
1 T	finely snipped parsley (optional)

In large mixing bowl, toss together the warm popcorn and the butter or margarine. Immediately sprinkle the Parmesan cheese, American cheese food, or taco seasoning and, if desired, the parsley. Toss to coat. Yield: 6 servings.

Taylor Whitney, Missoula, Montana

Nutty Cracker Delights

42	Keebler Club Crackers (2½ × 1 inch)
½ c	butter or margarine
½ c	sugar
1 tsp	vanilla extract
1 c	crushed almonds

Place crackers in a single layer in a foil-lined 15 × 10 × 1 inch baking dish. In a saucepan over medium heat, melt butter. Add sugar; bring to a boil, stirring constantly. Boil for 2 minutes. Remove from the heat; add vanilla. Pour evenly over crackers; sprinkle with nuts. Bake at 350° for 10 to 12 minutes or until lightly browned. Immediately remove from the pan, cutting between crackers if necessary, and cool on wire rack. Store in an airtight container. Yield: 3½ dozen.

Denise Riches, Irvine, California

Soups,
Breads,
Salads &
Side Dishes

**Great Accompaniments
for Delicious
Bunco Entrées**

Soups

Chilled Raspberry Soup

Great served as a first course for a luncheon. Leftover soup can be frozen for a yogurt-like snack.

1½ T	unflavored gelatin
⅓ c	cold water
¾ c	hot water
3 pkgs	frozen raspberries (10 oz), thawed
3½ c	sour cream (28 oz)
1⅓ c	pineapple juice
1⅓ c	half-and-half
1⅓ c	dry sherry
⅓ c	grenadine
2 T	lemon juice

Garnishes:

	mint
	whole raspberries

Soak gelatin in cold water for 5 minutes. Stir in hot water and dissolve over low heat. Push raspberries through a strainer to remove seeds, then puree. Combine with remaining ingredients and refrigerate overnight. Garnish with mint and/or whole raspberries. Yield: 12 servings.

Rachel Minor, Victoria, British Columbia

Cold Cucumber Soup

1 bch	green onions, sliced
2 T	butter
4 c	diced cucumbers
3 c	chicken broth
1 c	fresh spinach, chopped
½ c	potatoes, peeled and sliced
½ tsp	salt
1 T	lemon juice

pepper to taste
1 c   light cream
Garnishes:
radishes
green onions

In a saucepan, sauté green onions in butter until they are softened. Add cucumbers, chicken broth, spinach, potatoes, salt, lemon juice and pepper. Simmer uncovered until potatoes are tender. Transfer the mixture to a blender in batches and puree. Transfer the puree to a bowl and stir in the light cream. Let soup cool and chill for several hours, or overnight. Garnish each serving with slices of radishes and/or green onions. Yield: 8 servings.

Francis Ford, Fairbanks, Alaska

Gazpacho

3 lg	tomatoes, peeled and chopped
1	green bell pepper, chopped
1	cucumber, peeled and chopped
1 c	chopped celery
½ c	chopped green onion
4 c	tomato juice
2	avocados, chopped
5 T	red wine vinegar
4 T	olive oil
2 tsp	salt
½ tsp	black pepper

Garnishes:
sour cream
croutons

Be sure all vegetables are very finely chopped. Combine all ingredients in a large non-metallic bowl and chill overnight. Serve soup cold with a dollop of sour cream on top of each serving. Pass croutons in a bowl. Yield: 8 servings.

Alice Stevenson, Bakersfield, California

Bunco Night JOURNAL

Date of Party

Hostess

Party Theme

Menu

Winners

Who Else Played

Memories of the Evening

Creamy Clam and Broccoli Chowder

2 c	navy beans or small white beans
3 c	fat-free chicken broth (divided use)
1 tsp	olive oil
4 tsp	garlic, minced
2 c	small broccoli florets
2 cans	minced clams (6½ oz each), rinsed and drained
4	plum tomatoes, coarsely chopped
2 T	dry white wine
2 T	half-and-half
2 T	snipped fresh dill

In a food processor or using a handheld immersion blender, puree half the beans in ½ cup of the broth. Set mixture aside. Warm oil in a 4-quart pot over medium heat for 1 minute. Add garlic and sauté it for 1 minute. Add broccoli, remaining broth, remaining beans and bean puree; simmer broccoli until tender, about 4 minutes. Stir in clams. Heat mixture for 1 minute. Stir in tomatoes, wine, cream and dill. After stirring in cream, keep cooking to a minimum so cream doesn't curdle. Warm, then serve immediately. Yield: 4 servings.

Teri Williams, St. Paul, Minnesota

Cream Consommé

1 lg	onion, grated
1	tart apple, unpeeled and shredded
3 cans	beef consommé (10½ oz)
1½ c	heavy cream
½ tsp	paprika
½ tsp	curry powder
1	red apple, unpeeled and chopped, for garnish
2 T	fresh lemon juice

Add the shredded onion and apple to the consommé and cook until tender, about 12 minutes. Puree in a blender, then put through a strainer. Stir in cream and season with paprika and curry powder. Refrigerate until ready to serve. Reheat slowly, just until heated through. Serve in small cups garnished with chopped unpeeled apple sprinkled with lemon juice. Yield: 10 servings.

Helen McPheeters, Hollywood, California

Zucchini Squash Soup

¼ c	Crisco oil
1 c	onion, thinly sliced
2 tsp	garlic, minced
⅓ c	all-purpose flour
1 T	milk
8 c	chicken stock
5 c	sliced zucchini (2 pounds)
½ tsp	dried sweet basil
½ tsp	dried oregano
¼ tsp	pepper
1–2 c	half-and-half

Heat oil in heavy saucepan over medium low heat. Add onion and garlic and cook until onion is translucent, stirring occasionally, about 10 minutes. Combine flour with a little milk and mix. Stir with onions. Add stock, zucchini, pepper and herbs. Bring to a boil and simmer 30 minutes to 1 hour. Use Braun whisk or blender to blend smooth. Simmer another 20 minutes. Add half-and-half and simmer 20 more minutes.

Vera Riches, Thousand Oaks, California

Irish Stew

3 lb	lamb
4	onions
4	carrots
3 c	stock, water or wine
	salt and pepper
4	whole potatoes
	parsley, chopped

Cut fat from lamb and cube. Render fat in Dutch casserole. Brown lamb cubes in hot fat. Peel onions and carrots and cut into chunks. Add onions, carrots, liquid and seasonings. Peel whole potatoes and place them on top. Simmer gently for 1½ hours; turn occasionally to prevent sticking. Skim fat. Serve with a sprinkling of parsley and thicken liquid with arrowroot or flour.

Maureen Bailey, Boise, Idaho

Lentil Barley Soup

¾ c	onion, chopped
¾ c	celery, chopped
1	garlic clove, minced
¼ c	margarine
6 c	water
1 can	tomatoes (28 oz), cut up
¾ c	dry lentils, rinsed and drained
¾ c	pearl barley
6	vegetarian bouillon cubes
½ tsp	dried rosemary
½ tsp	dried oregano
¼ tsp	pepper
1 c	carrots, thinly sliced
1 c	cheese (Swiss, Parmesan, or Cheddar)

In a 4-quart Dutch oven, cook onion, celery and garlic in hot margarine until tender. Add water, undrained tomatoes, lentils, barley, bouillon cubes, rosemary, oregano and pepper. Bring to a boil;

reduce heat. Cover and simmer 45 minutes. Add carrots and simmer 15 minutes until carrots are tender. Serve and top with cheese. Yield: 5 servings.

Denise Riches, Irvine, California

Kidney Bean and Sausage Soup

1 lb	sausage (½ sweet and ½ hot)
1	large onion, chopped
2 cans	kidney beans (16 oz each)
1 can	crushed tomatoes (12 oz)
1	quart water
1	bay leaf
1 tsp	seasoned salt
½ tsp	garlic salt
½ tsp	thyme
⅛ tsp	pepper
½	green pepper, chopped
1 c	potatoes, cooked and diced

Remove casing from sausage and crumble in stockpot. Brown slightly with onion. Combine remaining ingredients except potatoes, add to pot and simmer one hour. Add potatoes and heat. Yield: 8 servings.

Sue Tillis, San Antonio, Texas

Enchilada Soup

3 cans	beef broth (14½ oz)
2 cans	stewed tomatoes (14½ oz)
1 can	La Palmas Enchilada Sauce (28 oz)
¾ c	onion, finely chopped
2	cloves garlic, minced
1 tsp	cumin
1 tsp	dried oregano leaves
¾ tsp	pepper
	vegetable oil
10	corn tortillas (6-inch), cut into pieces
8 oz	Monterey Jack Cheese, shredded

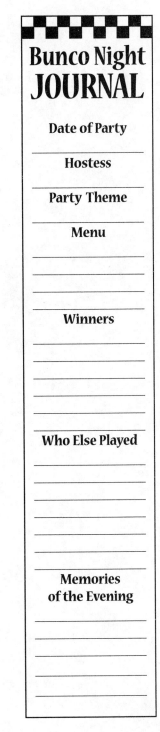

Bunco Night JOURNAL

Date of Party

Hostess

Party Theme

Menu

Winners

Who Else Played

Memories
of the Evening

In a large saucepan, combine all ingredients except oil, tortillas and cheese. Bring to a boil; reduce heat to low and simmer uncovered 30 minutes. Meanwhile, in a large skillet, heat oil. Add ¼ of the tortilla strips to the hot oil. Cook until crisp; remove with slotted spoon; drain on paper towel and repeat until all tortillas are cooked. To serve soup, place a generous handful of tortillas and some of the cheese in large individual soup bowls. Fill bowls with soup. Garnish with cheese and tortilla strips. Yield: 8 servings.

Lavon Campbell, El Paso, Texas

Breads and Muffins

Cheesy Herb Rolls

4   rolls (brown-and-serve or sourdough)
1 T   Parmesan cheese, shredded
¼ tsp   oregano

Preheat oven to 350°. Cut rolls in half; butter the cut sides. Sprinkle evenly with shredded cheese and oregano. Bake until rolls are lightly browned (approximately 10 minutes).
Yield: 4 servings.

Carol McAllister, Wichita, Kansas

Cheesy Bread Spread

1 c   sharp Cheddar cheese, shredded
1 c   mayonnaise
¾ c   onion, diced
1 tsp   horseradish
¼ tsp   garlic powder

Mix all ingredients together. Spread on French bread. Broil until golden brown.

Leslie Taylor, Fresno, California

Notes

Mozzarella Toast

3 T	butter, softened
1	clove garlic, minced
8 slices	French bread
8 slices	mozzarella
	dried basil
	oregano
	Lawry's Seasoned Salt

Combine butter and garlic. Spread butter mixture on bread and top with one slice of cheese. Lightly sprinkle with seasonings. Bake at 400° until cheese melts.

Kameryn Alexandra, Baltimore, Maryland

Scones

2 c	flour
1 tsp	baking powder
1 tsp	salt
1 tsp	sugar
4 T	butter
1	egg plus 1 yolk
½ c	milk

Sift dry ingredients. Add 1 egg and 1 yolk to milk. Beat. Add butter. Add to dry ingredients. Stir just to hold together. Knead on floured board. Pat into circle. Cut into triangles. Brush with egg white and sugar. Bake at 425° for 12 to 15 minutes. Serve with jam, honey or butter.

Ruby Blatmore, Miami, Florida

Zucchini Pineapple Muffins

3	eggs
1 c	oil
2 c	granulated sugar
2 tsp	vanilla
2 c	zucchini, coarsely shredded
1 can	crushed pineapple (8½ oz), well drained
3 c	flour
2 tsp	baking soda
1 tsp	salt
½ tsp	cinnamon
¾ tsp	nutmeg
1 c	chopped nuts or currants

Cream together the eggs, oil, sugar and vanilla. Stir in the zucchini and pineapple. In a separate bowl, combine the remaining ingredients. Stir the dry ingredients gently into the zucchini mixture until just blended. Pour into greased muffin cups or use paper muffin liners. Bake at 350° for 20 minutes. To make bread, grease and sugar two 5 × 9 inch loaf pans. Bake at 350° for 1 hour. Cool in pans for 10 minutes and then turn onto a rack.

Autumn Daniels, Palo Alto, California

Pumpkin Bread

3 c	sugar
1 c	oil
4	eggs
1½ tsp	salt
1 tsp	nutmeg
pinch	ground cloves
½ tsp	cinnamon
⅔ c	milk
2 c	pumpkin
3½ c	flour
2 T	soda
1 c	walnuts, chopped

Combine all ingredients together; beat well. Pour into two 9 × 5 × 3 inch loaf pans. Bake for 1½ hours at 350°.

Donna Thomas, Fremont, California

Monkey Bread

A sweet bread for brunch or serve it with Potato Quiche (page 64) for dinner.

⅔ c	sugar
2 tsp	cinnamon
3	tubes refrigerator biscuits
½ c	walnuts, chopped
¾ c	margarine
1 c	brown sugar

Mix white sugar with 1 teaspoon cinnamon. Cut each biscuit in quarters; roll in sugar mixture. Grease Bundt pan with nonstick cooking spray. Place walnuts in bottom of pan; add biscuits evenly over walnuts. Melt margarine, brown sugar and remaining cinnamon; pour over biscuits. Bake for 30 to 35 minutes at 350°. Cool 15 minutes before turning onto plate. Yield: 1 Bundt-pan-size loaf.

Donna Thomas, Fremont, California

Salads and Dressings

Creamy Lime Salad

4 c	liquid (some from crushed pineapple)
2 pkgs	lime Jell-O (small)
1 bag	miniature marshmallows
1 can	crushed pineapple (small)
1 c	sour cream
1 c	mayonnaise

Bunco Night JOURNAL

Date of Party

Hostess

Party Theme

Menu

Winners

Who Else Played

Memories of the Evening

Heat liquid to boiling. Add Jell-O and marshmallows gradually until dissolved. Add pineapple. Blend sour cream and mayonnaise together. Add some of the warm Jell-O mixture. Now blend all ingredients together. Pour into pan, refrigerate 3 to 4 hours.

Margaret Paul, Tuscon, Arizona

Cranberry Jell-O Salad

1 pkg   raspberry Jell-O (large)
1 can   whole cranberry sauce
1 can   crushed pineapple (large)
         chopped nuts

In a large glass dish, dissolve Jell-O in 1 cup boiling water. Add remaining ingredients, juice and all. Cover with plastic wrap and refrigerate overnight.

Donna Thomas, Fremont, California

Strawberry-Banana Jell-O Salad

1 pkg   strawberry-banana Jell-O (large)
2 c   water
1 can   whole cranberry sauce
1 pt   sour cream

Mix Jell-O and water together; stir until dissolved. Add cranberry sauce. Refrigerate until almost set; whip in sour cream. Refrigerate until completely set.

Angel Baca, Hanford, California

Chinese Chicken Salad

2   chicken breasts
         garlic salt
2   lettuce heads, shredded
3   green onions, chopped
½ c   almonds, sliced (toasted in skillet)

2 T	sesame seeds (toasted)
	fried Maifun (Chinese rice noodles) or
	Chun King brand chow mein crispy
	noodles
	cilantro (optional)
	mandarin oranges (optional)

Dressing:

5 T	sugar
1 tsp	salt
½ tsp	black salt
¼ c	peanut oil
2 tsp	sesame oil
3 T	white vinegar
2 T	mirin rice vinegar

Bake chicken at 350° for 45 minutes; season with garlic salt and shred. Mix remaining ingredients. Prepare dressing. Toss with salad.

Mia Fujii, Irvine, California

Spinach Salad

1 lb	bean sprouts
2 lb	spinach
2	hard-boiled eggs, sliced
8	large mushrooms, sliced
2	medium red onions, sliced
6	slices bacon, cooked and crumbled

Dressing:

⅔ c	oil
½ c	cider vinegar
¼ c	ketchup
3 T	honey
½ tsp	salt
1 tsp	dry mustard
1 tsp	celery seed
1 tsp	sesame oil
1 tsp	celery salt

All Cracked Up!

When boiling eggs, place a teaspoon of salt in the water to prevent cracking. If an egg does crack, pour in a little vinegar to keep the egg white from escaping.

Mix all the ingredients in a large salad bowl. Transfer to individual salad plates. Prepare dressing by simply blending all the ingredients together. Spoon dressing over top.

Pat Wale, Cypress, California

Monte Cristo Salad

Dressing:

1 c	mayonnaise
1 tsp	Dijon mustard
½ tsp	fresh tarragon, chopped, or ¼ tsp dried tarragon

Salad:

1 c	lobster meat, cubed and cooked
1 c	cooked potatoes, diced
1 c	mushrooms, sliced
1 c	Swiss cheese, coarsely shredded
4	hard-boiled eggs, coarsely chopped romaine lettuce
1	tomato, cut into wedges

Combine the dressing ingredients; mix well and chill. Combine the lobster, potatoes, mushrooms, cheese and eggs. Toss gently with the dressing and arrange neatly on leaves of romaine. Garnish with tomato wedges. Yield: 6 servings.

Patty Montgomery, Everett, Washington

Salad Nicoise

You can cook and chill the beans and potatoes for this French salad a day before serving.

½ lb	green beans
¾ lb	whole tiny new potatoes, scrubbed and sliced
¼ c	olive oil or salad oil
¼ c	white wine vinegar or white vinegar
1 tsp	sugar

1 tsp	snipped fresh tarragon or ¼ tsp dried tarragon, crushed
⅛ tsp	dry mustard
dash	pepper
	Boston or Bibb lettuce leaves
1½ c	flaked cooked tuna, or salmon (½ lb), or one can chunk white tuna (9¼ oz, water-packed), drained and broken into chunks
2	medium tomatoes, cut into wedges
2	hard-boiled eggs, sliced
½ c	pitted ripe olives (optional)
¼ c	thinly sliced green onions (2)
4	anchovy fillets, drained, rinsed and patted dry (optional)
	fresh chervil (optional)

Wash green beans; remove ends and string. In a large covered saucepan or pot, cook green beans and potatoes in a small amount of boiling water for 15 to 20 minutes or just until tender. Drain; place vegetables in a medium bowl. Cover and chill for 2 to 24 hours.

For dressing, in a screw-top jar, combine oil, vinegar, sugar, tarragon, dry mustard and pepper. Cover and shake well. To serve, line 4 salad plates with lettuce leaves. Arrange chilled vegetables, tuna or salmon, tomatoes, eggs, and if desired, olives on the lettuce-lined plates. Sprinkle each serving with green onions. If desired, top each salad with an anchovy fillet and garnish with chervil. Shake dressing well; pour some over each salad and serve. Yield: 4 main-dish servings.

Sonya Gordon, Boise, Idaho

Orange & Avocado Salad

¼ c	fresh orange juice
2 T	fresh lemon juice
2 tsp	olive oil
2 tsp	sugar
1 can	mandarin oranges (11 oz), drained

Bunco Night
JOURNAL

Date of Party

Hostess

Party Theme

Menu

Winners

Who Else Played

Memories of the Evening

¾ c	avocado, peeled and diced
½ c	red onion, sliced
3 c	green-leaf lettuce, tightly packed and torn

In a large bowl, whisk together the orange and lemon juices, olive oil and sugar. Stir in oranges, avocado and onion. Cover and refrigerate while flavors blend for at least 30 minutes. Add lettuce to chilled orange mixture and toss slightly. Yield: 6 servings.

Dody Fair, Newport Beach, California

Five-Bean Salad

1 can	kidney beans (1 lb)
1 can	broad beans (1 lb)
½ lb	white beans, soaked overnight
1 lb	fresh green beans
1 lb	fresh yellow beans
½ c	sour cream
¼ c	chopped parsley
½ c	oil
⅓ c	lemon juice
1 tsp	salt
pinch	pepper

Drain and rinse the canned beans. Drain the white beans. Blanch the green and yellow beans for 5 minutes. Mix the sour cream, parsley, oil, lemon juice, salt and pepper together. Toss the beans with the dressing and refrigerate for 3 hours. Yield: 8 servings.

Michael Tutor, Santa Barbara, California

Tropical Fruit Salad

¼ c	coconut, toasted (see below)
½ c	vanilla yogurt
1	ripe medium banana, cut up
2 T	pineapple juice

1	medium papaya, seeded, peeled and sliced
½	medium mango, seeded, peeled and chopped
2 c	honeydew melon and/or cantaloupe balls

Toast coconut in a shallow baking pan; bake at 350° for 5 to 10 minutes or until light golden brown, stirring once or twice. For dressing, combine yogurt, banana and pineapple juice in blender or food processor; cover and blend or process until smooth. Transfer to covered container and refrigerate while preparing fruit. Arrange the sliced papaya and chopped mango on 4 salad plates. Mound ½ cup of the melon balls atop each plate. Spoon 2 tablespoons dressing over each. Sprinkle each with 1 tablespoon of the toasted coconut. If desired, garnish with fresh mint sprigs. Yield: 4 side-dish servings.

Faith Williams, Austin, Texas

German-Style Potato Salad

4	medium potatoes (¼ lb) (For added color, use 12 small red potatoes.)
4	bacon slices
½ c	onion, chopped
1 T	all-purpose flour
1 T	sugar
½ tsp	salt
½ tsp	celery seed
½ tsp	dry mustard
¼ tsp	pepper
⅔ c	water
¼ c	vinegar
1	hard-boiled egg, chopped
2 T	fresh parsley or 2 slices bacon, crisp-cooked, drained and crumbled (optional)

Place potatoes in a saucepan; add water to cover and, if desired, ¼ teaspoon salt. Bring to boiling; reduce heat. Simmer, covered, until just tender; drain well. Cool potatoes slightly. Halve, peel and cut potatoes into ¼-inch-thick slices. Set aside. For dressing, in a large skillet, cook the four slices bacon over medium heat until crisp. Remove bacon, reserving 2 tablespoons drippings in skillet. Drain bacon on paper towels. Crumble the bacon and set aside. Add chopped onion to the reserved drippings. Cook over medium heat until tender. Stir in the flour, sugar, the ½ teaspoon salt, celery seed, dry mustard and pepper. Stir in the ⅔ cup water and vinegar. Cook, stirring gently, for 1 to 2 minutes more or until heated through. Transfer to a serving bowl. Garnish with egg and, if desired, parsley or crumbled bacon. Yield: 4 to 6 side-dish servings.

Kathy Samuels, Vail, Colorado

Chicken Taco Salad

2 T	olive oil
1 lb	skinless, boneless chicken breasts, cut into 1-inch pieces
½ tsp	salt
2 T	chili powder
1	medium head of iceberg lettuce, torn into bite-size pieces.
1 can	kidney beans (8 oz), rinsed and drained
1 can	sliced black olives (4 oz), drained
3	scallions, chopped
1 c	crushed tortilla chips
1 c	thick and chunky salsa
1 c	Cheddar cheese (about 4 oz), shredded
½ c	sour cream
1	large tomato, chopped
1	avocado, thinly sliced (optional)
¼ c	cilantro

In a medium skillet, heat oil over medium-high heat. Add chicken and cook, tossing, until white throughout, but still juicy, 3 to 4 minutes. Add salt and chili powder. Cook, stirring 1 minute to blend flavors. Remove from heat and set aside to cool slightly. (Chicken can be cooked ahead and refrigerated.)

In a large bowl, place lettuce, kidney beans, olives, scallions, tortilla chips, reserved chicken and salsa. Toss to mix. Divide salad among 4 plates. Top each with a quarter of cheese, sour cream, chopped tomato, avocado and cilantro. Yield: 4 servings.

Mary Wilcox, Sunnyvale, California

Pasta Seafood Salad

6	Tiger shrimp, butterflied
½ lb	multicolored rotini pasta
6	marinated artichoke hearts
2 T	capers
1 tsp	celery seeds
3 T	pimiento
1	red pepper, finely diced
½ lb	baby shrimp, cooked
1 can	salmon (7½ oz), drained
1 can	mini corn (8 oz)
2 oz	cashews

Dressing:

¼ c	raspberry dressing (any bottled dressing will do)
½ c	mayonnaise
½ c	heavy cream
2 T	powdered sugar
1 tsp	black pepper

Preheat oven to 350°. Bake Tiger shrimp in oven for 10 minutes. Cool. Boil pasta in salted water, al dente. Run under cold water until cool; drain well.

Place pasta in a large mixing bowl. Add the artichoke hearts, capers, celery seeds, pimiento and red pepper; toss well. Blend in the dressing. Arrange baby shrimp, salmon, Tiger shrimp, mini corn and cashews on top. Serve on individually chilled salad plates or as a buffet-style salad. Yield: 6 servings.

Faye Johnson, Auckland, New Zealand

Jessica's Pasta Salad

Prepare at least 6 to 8 hours ahead of time to let flavors blend. Adjust amount of ingredients depending on your crowd!

	tri-colored pasta (any shape)
	fresh tomato, cut into small pieces
	red and green peppers
1 can	black olives, sliced
	Bernstein's Italian Dressing

Optional ingredients:

artichoke hearts
Provolone cheese, diced
Parmesan cheese, shredded

Cook noodles until tender, rinse, drain and chill. Add remaining ingredients. Toss with enough dressing to coat well. Chill overnight.

Jessica Cassese, Irvine, California

Caesar Salad

The pumpernickel croutons add an unusual touch to this Caesar salad.

1	head romaine lettuce
1	egg, slightly beaten
2	garlic cloves, crushed
3 T	fresh lemon juice
½ c	olive oil
4	anchovy fillets, drained and chopped

2	hard-boiled eggs, peeled and quartered
½ c	Parmesan cheese, freshly shredded
¾ c	pumpernickel croutons
	fresh ground pepper

Croutons:

3 T	unsalted butter
3 T	mild olive oil
3 c	stale pumpernickel bread cubes (about ½-inch thick)
	garlic to taste
1 tsp	mixed herbs (parsley, chives, tarragon and chervil)
3 T	Parmesan cheese, shredded

For croutons: Heat butter and oil in large non-stick skillet over medium heat. Add the bread cubes and cook, tossing constantly with a wooden spoon, for 3 to 4 minutes. Reduce heat to medium low. Add the garlic and herbs. Continue to cook the croutons, tossing frequently, until golden brown, 20 to 25 minutes. Remove to a bowl and toss with Parmesan. Store in airtight container until ready to use. For salad: Rinse the lettuce and dry. Refrigerate wrapped in paper towels for several hours to crisp the leaves. Whisk the raw egg, garlic, lemon juice and oil together, and pour into the bottom of a large salad bowl. Add the lettuce, anchovies, and eggs, and toss gently. Add the cheese and toss again. Sprinkle with the croutons and serve immediately. Fresh ground pepper from the pepper mill adds the final touch to this delicious salad. Yield: 4 servings.

Paula Zimmer, Kansas City, Kansas

Caesar Salad Dressing

3	cloves garlic, quartered
½ tsp	salt
¼ c	Parmesan cheese
8	anchovy fillets, minced
2 T	Dijon style mustard
2 tsp	Worcestershire sauce
1 tsp	sugar
⅓ c	lemon juice, fresh
1 c	olive oil
2 T	parsley

Add first eight ingredients to food processor. Then add oil slowly. Refrigerate. Toss with cheese and croutons, then sprinkle with parsley.

Suzanne York, Van Nuys, California

Green Salad Dressing

1 c	Crisco oil
2 T	red wine vinegar
1 tsp	salt
1 tsp	sugar
1 tsp	parsley
¼ tsp	Tabasco
1	clove garlic, split in half

Mix ingredients. Store in an airtight container and refrigerate overnight for best flavor. Will keep for 2 to 3 weeks.

Vera Riches, Thousand Oaks, California

Ranch Dressing

½ c	buttermilk
1 c	mayonnaise
1 T	minced chives
1 T	lemon juice
¼ tsp	salt
pinch	white pepper

Fold the buttermilk into the mayonnaise. Whip in the remaining ingredients. Refrigerate. Yield: 2 cups.

Karen Foust, Spokane, Washington

1000 Island Dressing

1 c	mayonnaise
1/2 c	chili sauce
1/4 c	pickle relish
1/2 tsp	dry mustard
1/2 tsp	basil
1 T	pimiento
2	hard-boiled eggs, shredded

Blend all the ingredients together thoroughly. Refrigerate. Yield: 2 cups.

Karen Foust, Spokane, Washington

Poppy Seed Dressing

1½ c	French dressing (any bottled dressing will do)
1/3 c	sugar
2 T	poppy seeds

Blend the ingredients together thoroughly. Refrigerate. Yield: 2 cups.

Karen Foust, Spokane, Washington

Blue Cheese Dressing

1/4 c	blue cheese
1½ c	mayonnaise
1 T	lemon juice
1/2 tsp	salt
1/4 tsp	white pepper

Melt the cheese over a double boiler. Remove from heat and place in a mixing bowl. Fold in the mayonnaise, lemon juice and seasonings. If desired, crumble 1/2 cup blue cheese into prepared dressing. Yield: 2 cups.

Christine Morgan, Billings, Montana

**Bunco Night
JOURNAL**

Date of Party
_____

Hostess
_____

Party Theme
_____

Menu
_____
_____
_____
_____

Winners
_____
_____
_____
_____

Who Else Played
_____
_____
_____
_____
_____

**Memories
of the Evening**
_____
_____
_____
_____

Notes

Creamy Basil Dressing

2	shallots, minced
2 T	fresh basil, minced
1 tsp	Dijon mustard
½ c	olive oil
¼ tsp	salt
¼ tsp	pepper
3 T	lemon juice

Combine the shallots, basil, mustard, oil, salt and pepper in a blender or food processor. With the machine running, slowly pour in the lemon juice. Use as a salad dressing or as a marinade. Yield: 1 cup.

Vickie Rice, Portland, Oregon

Honey Lemon Dressing

1 btl	French dressing (any bottled variety)
¼ c	honey
2 T	lemon juice
1 tsp	ground cinnamon

Blend together the dressing, honey, lemon juice and cinnamon thoroughly. Refrigerate.

Vickie Rice, Portland, Oregon

Fresh Tomato Dressing

1 c	fresh tomatoes, peeled, seeded and chopped
¼ c	honey
1 tsp	Worcestershire sauce
½ tsp	dry mustard
1 tsp	salt
2 tsp	oregano
½ tsp	fresh-cracked black pepper
3 T	lemon juice
¼ c	vinegar
¾ c	safflower oil

Place all ingredients into a blender or food processor. Blend for 1 minute or until a smooth sauce is formed. Refrigerate. Yield: 2 cups.

Cory Miller, Wichita, Kansas

Green Goddess Dressing

1 oz	anchovy paste
1	garlic clove, minced
2	green onions, chopped
1 T	parsley flakes
1 T	chopped tarragon
1 T	chopped chives
2	egg yolks
2 c	oil
¼ c	lemon juice

In a blender, puree the anchovy paste, garlic, green onions, parsley, tarragon and chives. Add the egg yolks. With the blender running, slowly pour in the oil. Add lemon juice. Use for salads or chicken. Yield: 2½ cups.

Taylor Coldwell, London, England

Side Dishes

Corn Pudding

1 can	whole kernel corn (12 oz), drained
1 can	cream-style corn (16 oz)
2	eggs, beaten
8 oz	sour cream
1 stk	margarine or butter, melted
1 box	Jiffy corn muffin mix (small)

Mix all ingredients except Jiffy mix and place in refrigerator overnight. When ready to bake, stir in box of Jiffy mix. Bake at 350° for 60 to 70 minutes, or until firm when lightly shaken. Yield: 6 to 8 servings.

Sue McClean, Dallas, Texas

Broccoli Casserole

1 pkg	frozen broccoli, chopped
¼ c	onion, minced
½ c	cream of mushroom soup
½ c	mayonnaise
1	egg
½ c	sharp Cheddar cheese, shredded
	Ritz crackers or 1 can Durkee Onion Rings

Cook broccoli and drain. Mix other ingredients together and add to broccoli. Cover with crushed crackers or onion rings. Bake at 375° for 30 minutes. Yield: 4 to 6 servings.

Abigail Conners, Mobile, Alabama

Corn Vegetable Medley

1 can	Campbell's Golden Corn Soup
½ c	milk
2 c	broccoli pieces
1 c	carrots, sliced
1 c	cauliflower pieces
½ c	Cheddar cheese, shredded

In a saucepan, bring soup and milk to a boil, stirring often; stir in vegetables. Return to boiling. Cover and cook over low heat 20 minutes or until vegetables are tender. Keep stirring. Add cheese and heat through. Yield: 6 servings.

Jody Wither, Anchorage, Alaska

Sautéed Zucchini

1 T	salad oil
3	medium zucchini (about 1 lb) sliced
¼ tsp	Italian herb seasoning or basil
¼ tsp	salt
	dash pepper
1 T	water

In a large skillet, heat oil. Add zucchini, herbs, salt and pepper. Stir until zucchini is well coated. Add water; cover and simmer 5 minutes or until zucchini is tender.

Denise Riches, Irvine, California

Baked Fresh Vegetables

This easy, no-fuss recipe adjusts easily to make a small amount of vegetables or enough for a party. Simply adapt it to your needs.

> broccoli
> cauliflower
> carrots
> onion, sliced
> zucchini
> green beans
> snow peas
> or any other vegetables you like
> vegetable seasoning to taste
> garlic salt to taste
> lemon pepper to taste
> butter

Wash vegetables thoroughly and cut into bite-size pieces. Spray a large casserole dish with nonstick cooking spray. Place vegetables in dish and sprinkle with vegetable seasoning, garlic salt and pepper. Divide up ¼ to ½ cup butter, depending on the amount of vegetables and distribute over vegetables. Cover and bake at 350° for 45 minutes to 1 hour, stirring several times. If pan becomes dry, add more butter. Yield: 12 servings.

Candice Gordon, Leucadia, California

Bunco Night
JOURNAL

Date of Party

Hostess

Party Theme

Menu

Winners

Who Else Played

**Memories
of the Evening**

Notes

Spinach Ring

A great holiday side dish.

2 pkgs frozen chopped spinach, drained
2 pkgs cream cheese with chives (3 oz each),
        softened
1 can   mushroom soup (10¾ oz)
2   eggs

Grease Jell-O ring mold. Preheat oven to 350°. Combine all ingredients in blender. Mix well and pour in mold. Set mold in pan of water to cook. Bake for 50 minutes. Invert onto a platter. Serve with cooked carrots as garnish in the center of the ring.

Emily Borden, Detroit, Michigan

Potato Casserole

¼ c   butter, melted
1 can cream of chicken soup
2 c   sour cream
2 c   Cheddar cheese, shredded
2 T   onion, chopped
24 oz frozen hash browns, shredded or cubed
       and thawed (You may substitute fresh
       potatoes for the frozen hash browns;
       parboiled and diced.)
1 can Durkee's Fried Onions

Melt butter and pour into 9 x 13 inch pan. Set aside ½ cup cheese and Durkee's onions. Stir together remaining ingredients and turn into baking dish. Top with remaining cheese and onions. Bake at 350° for 50 to 60 minutes.

Sandy Johnson, Jacksonville, Oregon

Bunco
Entrées

**Crowd-Pleasing
Bunco Entrées
Your Guests
Will Love**

Chicken Tortilla Casserole

1 can	cream of mushroom soup
1 can	cream of chicken soup
1 c	sour cream
1 can	sliced black olives (small can)
1 can	diced green chilies (small can)
1	onion, medium size
12	corn tortillas, broken into bite-size pieces
5–6	chicken breasts, cooked and cubed
2 c	Cheddar cheese, shredded

Spray a 9 × 13 inch baking dish with cooking spray. Mix the soup, sour cream, olives, chilies and onion together. Layer half of the tortillas in bottom of pan, then half the chicken, then half the sauce, then half the cheese and repeat. Bake at 350° about 30 minutes or until heated through. Yield: 10 to 12 servings.

Denise Riches, Irvine, California

Chicken Divan

2 pkgs	frozen broccoli or 1 bunch fresh
2 c	chicken, cooked and cubed
1 can	cream of chicken soup
½ c	mayonnaise
½ c	sour cream
1 T	lemon juice
½ tsp	curry powder
1 c	Cheddar cheese, shredded
1 T	melted butter
½ c	soft bread crumbs

Cook and drain broccoli; place in a 9 × 13 inch greased pan. Place chicken in pan. Mix soup, mayonnaise, sour cream, lemon juice and curry; pour over chicken. Top with cheese. In a separate bowl, combine melted butter and bread crumbs; toss to coat. Add to top of cheese. Bake at 350° for 30 minutes. Yield: 12 servings.

Donna Thomas, Fremont, California

Creamed Chicken Casserole

Great for leftover chicken or turkey.

3	chicken breasts
	celery and onions
1 c	sour cream (or plain yogurt)
1 can	cream of mushroom soup
¼ lb	butter (1 stick)
1 pkg	Pepperidge Farm Stuffing Mix (8 oz)
1 c	chicken broth

Stew chicken in salted water, celery and onion for 45 minutes. Cool and cube meat, retaining one cup of broth. Mix soup and sour cream. Add cubed chicken. Mix melted butter, stuffing and broth. Put a layer of the stuffing mix on the bottom of a greased casserole dish; then add chicken mixture, ending with a layer of stuffing mixture on top. Bake at 350° for 45 minutes.

Elizabeth Guenther, Lakewood, California

Tamale Pie

1	large onion, chopped
1½ lb	ground beef
3	large tamales, cut up
2 cans	tomato sauce
1 can	cream-style corn
1 can	pitted black olives
	salt and pepper
2 c	Jack cheese

Brown onion and meat; combine with other ingredients except cheese and turn into a casserole dish. Cover with thick slices of Jack cheese. Bake, covered, at 350° for 1 hour. Keep casserole covered first 30 to 40 minutes of baking. Serve with cornbread and honey butter. To prepare honey butter, mix softened butter with an electric mixer until creamy. Add honey to taste. Transfer to a serving dish. Yield: 8 servings.

Lynn Robertson, Irvine, California

Bunco Night JOURNAL

Date of Party

Hostess

Party Theme

Menu

Winners

Who Else Played

Memories of the Evening

Potato Quiche

Great for brunch or dinner! Serve with Monkey Bread (page 43). You can make this recipe the day before and add the eggs and milk before baking.

16 oz	frozen hash browns (small cubed variety)
2 T	margarine, melted
4 oz	Monterey Jack cheese, shredded
4 oz	mild Cheddar cheese, shredded
12 oz	sausage, cooked and crumbled
3	eggs, slightly beaten
1 can	evaporated milk, small

Line casserole dish with frozen potatoes, drizzle with margarine and bake for 25 minutes at 450°. Sprinkle cheeses over hash browns; add cooked sausage. Mix eggs and evaporated milk; pour over sausage. Bake at 350° for 30 minutes.

Sandy Johnson, Jacksonville, Oregon

Tex-Mex Chicken Casserole

1 c	onion, chopped
2 T	margarine, butter or olive oil
1 pkg	Chicken Rice-A-Roni mix (7 oz)
1 c	white rice
2 cans	chicken broth (14 oz)
2½ c	water
4 c	cooked chicken or turkey, cut into small pieces
4	medium tomatoes, chopped
1 can	green chilies (4 oz), diced and drained
2 T	dried basil
1 T	chili powder
¼ tsp	ground cumin
¼ tsp	pepper
1 c	Cheddar cheese, shredded

In a 3-quart saucepan, cook onion in hot margarine until tender; stir in rice mix, seasoning packet and white rice. Cook and stir for 2 minutes. Stir in broth and water. Bring to a boil; reduce heat. Cover and simmer 20 minutes (liquid will not be fully absorbed). Transfer to a large mixing bowl; add chicken, tomato, chilies, basil, chili powder, cumin and pepper. Transfer to a 3-quart casserole dish. Bake covered at 425° for 20 minutes. Uncover, sprinkle with cheese and bake another 5 minutes. Yield: 12 servings.

Faye Johnson, Auckland, New Zealand

Western Meal-in-One

1 lb	ground beef
1 T	vegetable oil
1	clove garlic, minced
½ c	onion, chopped
½ c	green pepper, chopped
1 tsp	salt
1 tsp	chili powder
1 can	red beans (16 oz), drained
2½ c	tomatoes with juice, chopped and drained
2 c	cooked rice
¾ c	Cheddar cheese, shredded
¼ c	black olives, sliced

Brown ground beef in oil with garlic. Add the onion and green pepper; cook until onion is transparent. Drain off fat. In a 2-quart casserole dish, combine the meat mixture, salt, chili powder, beans, tomatoes and rice. Bake uncovered at 350° for 30 minutes. Sprinkle with cheese and olives; bake for 15 minutes more. Yield: 6 to 8 servings.

Faith Williams, Austin, Texas

Sausage and Cheese Casserole

8 slices white bread (without crust and cubed)
1½ lb cooked link sausage
¾ lb Cheddar cheese, shredded
4 eggs
3 c milk
¾ tsp dry mustard
½ tsp salt
1 can Cheddar cheese soup (undiluted)

Coat a 9 x 13 inch baking dish with nonstick cooking spray. Layer bread and sausage, top with cheese. Mix and beat the eggs, 2½ cups of the milk, dry mustard and the salt. Pour over bread mixture; cover with foil and refrigerate overnight. Before baking, mix Cheddar cheese soup with ½ cup of milk and pour over cold casserole. Bake at 300° for 1½ hours uncovered. Let sit approximately 15 to 20 minutes before serving. Yield: 10 to 12 servings.

Morgan Hansen, Northridge, California

Mexican Fritos

Sauce:
1 small onion, chopped
1 garlic clove
1 lb ground beef
1 can tomato sauce
1 can tomato paste
3 cans water
3 T sugar
1 tsp oregano
1 tsp chili powder
1 tsp cumin
1 tsp salt
1 c corn chips

Toppings:

    shredded cheese
    chopped lettuce
    avocado
    tomato
    green onions
    sliced black olives
    sour cream

Sauté onion and garlic; add ground beef and rest of sauce ingredients. Cook over low heat for 40 minutes. To serve, place 1 cup of corn chips on plate, ladle sauce over chips, layer with topping ingredients. Yield: 6 servings.

Edith Cramer, Tustin, California

Cheese Soufflé

8 c	*day-old bread cubes*
2 c	*Cheddar cheese, shredded*
¼ tsp	*pepper*
2 c	*milk*
2 T	*butter*
2 tsp	*Dijon-style mustard*
5	*eggs*
1 tsp	*salt*
	pinch cayenne pepper
1 tsp	*Parmesan cheese*

Spread half the bread in a greased 9-inch square baking dish. Sprinkle with half the Cheddar cheese. Season with half the pepper. Repeat layers with remaining bread, cheese and pepper. In a small saucepan, warm milk and butter over medium heat until butter melts and little bubbles form around the edge of the pan. Blend in mustard. In a large bowl, beat eggs. Stir in milk mixture, salt and cayenne. Pour evenly over bread mixture. Sprinkle with Parmesan. Let stand for 10 minutes to soften bread. Bake at 350° for 35 minutes, or until crisp, golden and puffed. Yield: 4 servings.

Karen Lundquist, New York City, New York

Bunco Night JOURNAL

Date of Party

Hostess

Party Theme

Menu

Winners

Who Else Played

**Memories
of the Evening**

Notes

Corned Beef Dinner

1	corned beef brisket (3 to 4 lb)
	water
½ c	onion, chopped
2	cloves garlic
2	bay leaves
6	medium potatoes, peeled
6	small carrots
6	cabbage wedges
1 tsp	prepared mustard
3 T	brown sugar
	dash of ground cloves

Place meat in Dutch oven; add water (about 7 cups) to cover. Add onion, garlic and bay leaves. Cover; simmer 3 to 4 hours or until tender. Remove meat. Add potatoes and carrots to simmering liquid. Cover and bring to a boil; cook 5 minutes. Add cabbage; cook 25 minutes more until vegetables are tender. Meanwhile, place meat, fat side up, in shallow pan. Spread with mustard; sprinkle with mixture of sugar and cloves. Bake at 350° for 15 minutes. Serve meat with vegetables; spoon simmering liquid over top. Yield: 6 to 8 servings.

Marissa Brown, Memphis, Tennessee

Egg Fondue

Another great recipe for brunch!

12	white bread slices (crust removed)
	butter
1 c	Cheddar cheese
1 can	diced green chilies
7	eggs
4 c	milk
	salt and pepper to taste

Spray a 9 x 13 inch pan with nonstick cooking spray. Butter one side of bread (six slices) and place in pan, butter side down. Layer with

cheese and chilies. Top with remaining bread, butter side up. In a bowl, mix eggs, milk, salt and pepper. Pour over bread. Cover with foil and let sit in
fridge overnight. Cook covered, at 400° for 1¼
hours. Let sit before serving. Yield: 12 servings.

Donna Rubio, Johnston, Rhode Island

Chili and Corn Soufflé

Great accompaniment to enchiladas and beans.

1 c	Bisquick
1 can	creamed corn (16 oz)
½ c	milk
1 T	butter, melted
1 T	sugar
1 can	diced green chilies
	Jack cheese, sliced

Mix together Bisquick, corn, milk, butter and
sugar. Spray a 13 × 13 inch square baking
dish with nonstick cooking spray. Pour in half the
batter, then sprinkle with chilies and cheese. Pour
remaining batter on top. Bake at 400° for 40 to
45 minutes.

Julie Wilson, Cleveland, Ohio

Fried Buttermilk Chicken

Make this chicken the day before and serve it cold,
or warm it in the oven just before guests arrive.

1 c	Crisco oil
8	chicken breasts, cut in half
⅔ c	buttermilk
¾ c	all-purpose flour
1 tsp	salt
1 tsp	onion powder
¼ tsp	pepper

In a large skillet, heat oil over medium-high heat.
Place chicken in bowl; pour buttermilk over
chicken and turn to coat each piece. Combine dry

Uses for Leftover Chili

Top baked potatoes with leftover chili.

Great over hot cooked noodles or mixed with white rice.

Spoon over corn chips for a tasty snack.

Use it as a classic hot-dog topper.

Cornbread or biscuits make a wonderful bed for topping with chili.

Spoon onto noodles, top with cheese and bake.

Wrap it up in a warm flour tortilla or pita bread.

Mix with melted cream cheese or processed cheese for a tortilla chip dip.

---

ingredients in paper or plastic bag; add chicken and shake until well coated. Add chicken to pan and cook until lightly browned, turning frequently. Reduce heat to low, cover and cook 20 minutes, turning occasionally. Remove cover; cook over medium-high heat 3 minutes more to crisp. Drain on paper towel. Yield: 8 servings.

Paulette Porter, Raleigh, North Carolina

Turkey Chili

1½	large onions, chopped
3	cloves garlic, crushed
2 T	olive oil
2 lb	ground turkey
2 T	chili powder
3 tsp	salt
2 cans	diced tomatoes (16 oz each)
1 can	stewed tomatoes (12 oz)
2 cans	pinto beans (16 oz each)
2 tsp	cumin
2 tsp	oregano
2 cans	corn, or 1 pkg frozen
2 tsp	cocoa
1 tsp	red pepper sauce

Sauté onion and garlic in oil. Add turkey and brown. Add rest of ingredients; simmer 1 hour. Yield: 6 to 8 servings.

Ginny White, Minneapolis, Minnesota

Chicken and Broccoli Stir Fry

1½ lb	chicken, skin removed and cut into bite-size pieces
1 T	canola oil
2	medium bunches of broccoli
1 pkg	fresh mushrooms, washed and sliced
1 c	chicken broth

2 T	soy sauce
1 T	sesame oil
¼ tsp	ground ginger
1 T	cornstarch
	water

Cook chicken in canola oil in a wok or skillet until no longer pink. Add broccoli, mushrooms, broth, soy sauce, sesame oil and ginger; cook until vegetables are tender. Stir frequently. Mix cornstarch with water until creamy. Add to pan and cook until thickened. Serve over white rice. Yield: 5 servings.

DeAnna McKelvie, Huntington Beach, California

Taco Salad

1 lb	ground beef
1 pkg	Lawry's taco seasoning mix
1	head of lettuce, chopped or shredded
1 can	black beans, drained and rinsed
1 can	white corn, drained
	fresh tomatoes, cut up into small pieces
1 pkg	Mexican-style shredded cheese
	tortilla chips, crumbled into bite-size pieces
	ranch dressing
1 can	black olives, sliced (optional)
	avocado (optional)

Cook beef according to taco seasoning mix directions. Let cool. Mix together meat, lettuce, black beans, corn, tomatoes, cheese and chips. Toss until well mixed. Add ranch dressing and toss to evenly coat salad. Top with olives or chunks of avocado if desired. Serve immediately. Yield: 10 to 12 servings.

Jessica Cassese, Irvine, California

Spinach Chicken Salad

5 c	chicken, cooked and cubed (about three whole breasts)
2 c	green grapes, cut into halves
1 c	snow peas
2 c	fresh spinach, torn
2½ c	sliced celery
7 oz	corkscrew pasta, cooked and drained
1 jar	marinated artichoke hearts, drained and quartered
1	medium cucumber, sliced
3	green onions with tops, sliced

Dressing:

½ c	vegetable oil
¼ c	sugar
2 T	white wine vinegar
1 tsp	salt
½ tsp	dried minced onions
1 tsp	lemon juice
2 T	fresh parsley, minced

In a large bowl, combine the chicken, grapes, peas, spinach, celery, pasta, artichoke hearts, cucumber and green onions. Cover and refrigerate. Combine all dressing ingredients in a jar or small bowl; mix well and refrigerate. Just before serving, pour dressing over salad and toss. If desired, serve on a spinach leaf and garnish with orange slices. Yield: 8 to 10 servings.

Morgan Hansen, Northridge, California

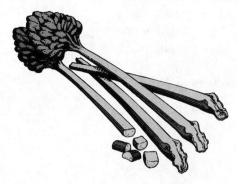

Lasagna

Sauce:

2¼ lb	ground beef
1 lb	Italian sausage
3	onions, finely diced
1	green pepper, finely diced
4 oz	mushrooms, sliced
2	celery stalks, finely diced
2 T	olive oil
2 c	tomatoes, seeded and chopped
½ c	tomato paste
2 tsp	salt
1 tsp	pepper
1 tsp	garlic powder
1 tsp	rosemary
1 tsp	oregano
1 tsp	basil
1 tsp	thyme
1 lb	lasagna noodles
1 lb	cottage cheese
1½ lb	mozzarella cheese, shredded
1 lb	Cheddar cheese, shredded
1 c	Parmesan cheese, shredded

Brown meats together with vegetables in the oil. Add tomatoes and tomato paste; simmer for 15 minutes. Add seasonings, reduce heat and simmer for 2 hours. Cook noodles al dente.

Preheat oven to 350°. Grease a 15 x 10 x 2 inch casserole or baking dish. Layer noodles, cottage cheese, sauce, shredded mozzarella and Cheddar cheese. Finish so that shredded cheese is on top. Sprinkle with Parmesan cheese. Bake in oven for 45 to 50 minutes. Remove, slice and serve. Yield: 10 to 12 servings.

Julie Wilson, Cleveland, Ohio

Bunco Night JOURNAL

Date of Party

_____

Hostess

_____

Party Theme

_____

Menu

_____
_____
_____
_____

Winners

_____
_____
_____
_____
_____

Who Else Played

_____
_____
_____
_____
_____

Memories of the Evening

_____
_____
_____
_____
_____

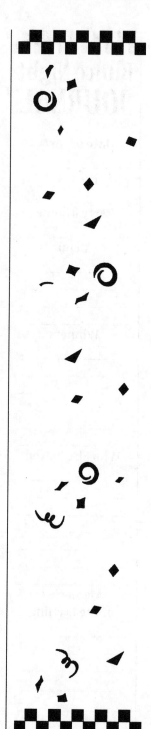

Spinach Manicotti

8	dried manicotti shells
¼ c	sliced green onions
1	clove garlic, minced
2 T	margarine or butter
2 T	all-purpose flour
1⅓ c	milk
1 c	Swiss cheese, shredded
¼ c	dry white wine or chicken broth
1	egg
1 pkg	frozen chopped spinach (10 oz), thawed and well drained
½ c	ricotta cheese
½ c	Parmesan cheese, shredded
½ c	crumbled feta cheese
¼ tsp	finely grated lemon peel
⅛ tsp	ground nutmeg

Cook manicotti about 18 minutes or until tender but still firm. Drain well. Cool manicotti in a single layer on a piece of greased foil. Meanwhile, for sauce, in a saucepan, cook green onions and garlic in margarine or butter until tender. Stir in flour. Add milk all at once. Cook and stir until thick and bubbly. Add Swiss cheese and wine or chicken broth, stirring until cheese melts. For filling, in a mixing bowl, stir together egg, spinach, ricotta cheese, Parmesan cheese, feta cheese, lemon peel and nutmeg. Use a small spoon to fill manicotti shells with filling. Arrange filled shells in a 2-quart rectangular baking dish. Pour sauce over filled shells. Bake, covered, at 350° for 35 to 40 minutes or until heated through. Serve. Yield: 4 servings.

Jan Danato, Tampa, Florida

One-Pot Spaghetti

This easy spaghetti lets you cook the pasta right in the sauce!

8 oz	ground beef or pork sausage
1 c	sliced fresh mushrooms or one jar sliced mushrooms (6 oz), drained
½ c	chopped onion
1	clove garlic, minced, or ⅛ tsp garlic powder
1 can	chicken broth or beef broth (14½ oz)
1¾ c	water
1 can	tomato paste (6 oz)
1 tsp	dried oregano, crushed
½ tsp	dried basil or marjoram, crushed
¼ tsp	pepper
6 oz	dried spaghetti, broken
¼ c	Parmesan cheese, shredded

In a large saucepan, cook the ground beef or pork sausage, fresh mushrooms (if using), onion and garlic until meat is brown and onion is tender. Drain fat. Stir in the canned mushrooms (if using), chicken or beef broth, water, tomato paste, oregano, basil or marjoram and pepper. Bring to a boil. Add the broken spaghetti, a little at a time, stirring constantly. Return to boil; reduce heat. Boil gently, uncovered, for 17 to 20 minutes or until spaghetti is tender and sauce is of the desired consistency, stirring frequently. Serve with Parmesan cheese. Yield: 4 servings.

Dee Kemper, Nashville, Tennessee

Baked Ravioli With Meat Sauce

8 oz	ground beef, ground pork or bulk pork sausage
½ c	carrot, finely chopped
⅓ c	onion, chopped (1 small)
1	clove garlic, minced
1 can	diced tomatoes (14½ oz)
1 c	water or ¾ c water and ¼ c red wine
1 can	tomato paste (6 oz)

½ c	fully cooked ham, diced or crisp-cooked bacon, crumbled
2 tsp	sugar
2 tsp	dried Italian seasoning, crushed
¼ tsp	pepper
½ pkg	frozen cheese-filled ravioli (27½- or 30-oz package or one 15- or 16-oz package frozen cheese-filled tortellini)
1 c	mozzarella cheese, shredded

For meat sauce, in a large skillet, cook ground meat, carrot, onion and garlic until meat is brown and onion is tender. Drain fat. Stir in undrained tomatoes, water, tomato paste, ham or bacon, sugar, Italian seasoning and pepper. Bring to a boil; reduce heat. Simmer, uncovered, for 5 minutes, stirring occasionally. Spoon ⅓ of the meat sauce into a 2-quart square baking dish. Arrange frozen ravioli or tortellini atop the meat sauce. Sprinkle with ½ cup of the mozzarella cheese. Top with the remaining meat sauce. Bake, covered, at 350° for 40 to 45 minutes or until pasta is tender. Uncover and sprinkle with remaining mozzarella cheese. Bake about 5 minutes more or until cheese melts. Yield: 6 main-dish servings.

Louise Sanderson, Richmond, Virginia

Pesto for Pasta

For a tasty appetizer, you can use this wonderful sauce to spread on thinly sliced pieces of French bread, sprinkled with Parmesan cheese and toasted. It's heavenly!

1 c	firmly packed fresh basil leaves
½ c	firmly packed fresh parsley sprigs with stems removed or torn fresh spinach
½ c	Parmesan or Romano cheese, shredded
¼ c	pine nuts, walnuts, or almonds
1 lg	clove garlic, quartered
¼ tsp	salt

¼ c	olive oil or cooking oil
12 oz	dried fettuccine (spaghetti can be substituted)

In a blender or food processor bowl, combine basil, parsley, Parmesan or Romano cheese, nuts, garlic and salt. Cover and blend or process with several on-off turns until a paste forms, stopping the machine several times and scraping the sides. With the machine running slowly, gradually add olive oil or cooking oil and blend or process to the consistency of soft butter. Cook fettuccine 8 to 10 minutes, or until tender but still firm. Drain well. Return fettuccine to pot. Toss pesto with fettuccine. Serve immediately. Yield: 12 side-dish servings.

Patricia Conan, Lincoln, Nebraska

Fresh Tomato Pasta Sauce

2	large ripe tomatoes
4 T	olive oil
¼ c	fresh basil leaves, chopped
¼ c	scallions, chopped
1 T	fresh oregano leaves, chopped
2	garlic cloves, minced
¼ tsp	salt
	freshly ground pepper to taste
	freshly grated Parmesan cheese

Blanch tomatoes in boiling water for 30 seconds. Then plunge the tomatoes into cold water; drain and peel. Cut tomatoes in half, remove seeds, drain off juices and dice. Combine the diced tomatoes with 2 tablespoons of the olive oil in a mixing bowl. Add the remaining ingredients, except the cheese, and toss to blend. To serve, toss pasta with remaining olive oil, top with sauce and grated Parmesan cheese. Yield: 2 cups.

Jennifer Santillo, Valencia, California

Bunco Night JOURNAL

Date of Party

Hostess

Party Theme

Menu

Winners

Who Else Played

Memories of the Evening

Fettuccine Alfredo

Accompany this with our Caesar Salad and Cheesy Herb Rolls and there you have it! A Bunco night to remember.

⅓ c	half-and-half, light cream or whipping cream
1 T	margarine or butter
4 oz	dried spinach or plain fettuccine
⅓ c	Parmesan cheese, shredded
	cracked black pepper
	ground nutmeg

Allow half-and-half and margarine to stand at room temperature for 30 minutes. Meanwhile, cook fettuccine 8 to 10 minutes, or until tender but still firm. Drain. Return fettuccine to warm saucepan; add half-and-half, margarine and Parmesan cheese. Toss gently until fettuccine is well coated. Transfer to a warm serving dish. Sprinkle with pepper and nutmeg and serve immediately. Yield: 4 side-dish servings.

Sandi Newhart, Bismarck, North Dakota

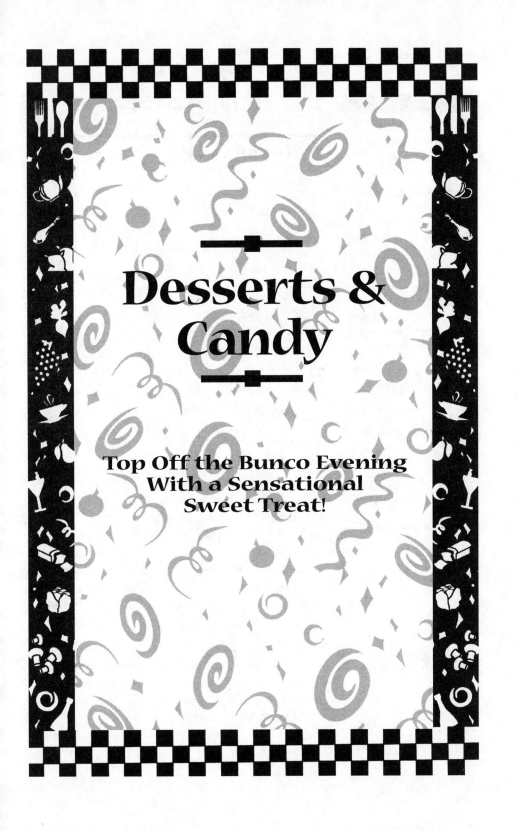

Desserts & Candy

**Top Off the Bunco Evening
With a Sensational
Sweet Treat!**

Desserts

Oatmeal Cake

1 c	oatmeal
1½ c	boiling water
½ c	butter
1 c	sugar
1 c	brown sugar, firmly packed
2	eggs
1 tsp	vanilla
1⅓ c	flour
1 tsp	baking soda
½ tsp	salt
1 tsp	cinnamon
½ tsp	nutmeg

Icing:

6 T	margarine, melted
1 c	brown sugar
1 c	coconut
½ c	nuts
2 T	milk

Mix oatmeal with boiling water; let stand 20 minutes. Meanwhile, cream together the butter and sugars. Add eggs and vanilla; mix well. Add oatmeal mixture. In a separate bowl, sift together flour, soda, salt, cinnamon and nutmeg. Stir flour mixture into egg mixture. Beat about 2 minutes, then turn into a greased 9 × 12 inch cake pan. Bake at 350° about 30 minutes.

Prepare icing by mixing melted margarine with remaining ingredients. While cake is still warm, spread icing over top and place under broiler only a minute or two, until bubbly. DO NOT BURN! Yield: 10 to 12 servings.

Chris Landers, Palmdale, California

Four-Layer Dessert

1	Jiffy cake mix (white or yellow)
1 pkg	cream cheese, softened (8 oz)
1 pkg	vanilla instant pudding
1 can	crushed pineapple, large
1 container	Cool Whip
	chopped nuts

Bake cake in a 9 x 13 inch pan for 20 to 23 minutes until it shrinks away from sides of pan. Watch carefully; cool. Beat cream cheese until smooth. Take the milk called for in the pudding and blend with cheese. Then add pudding mix and beat for 2 minutes. Spread on cooled cake. Drain pineapple thoroughly. Spread over pudding. Cover with Cool Whip and chill. Sprinkle with chopped nuts. Yield: 12 servings.

Brenda Loomis, Lakewood, California

Carrot Cake

2 c	flour
2 tsp	baking powder
1½ tsp	baking soda
1 tsp	salt
1 tsp	cinnamon
2 c	sugar
1½ c	vegetable oil
4	eggs
2 c	carrots, grated
1 can	crushed pineapple (8 oz), drained
1 c	walnuts, chopped

Frosting:

½ c	butter
8 oz	cream cheese
1 tsp	vanilla
1 lb	powdered sugar, sifted

Quick Tip

**If you need softened but-
ter** in a hurry, grate it.

Sift the flour, powder, soda, salt and cinnamon together. Add sugar, oil and eggs; mix well. Add carrots, pineapple and nuts; blend well. Pour into 3 greased 9-inch layer pans or a 10 × 14 × 2 inch cake pan. Bake at 350° for 35 to 40 minutes. Cool and turn out onto platter. Frost when completely cool.

To make frosting, cream together butter and cream cheese. Add vanilla and powdered sugar. Add drops of milk if too thick.

Porter Reece, Pittsburgh, Pennsylvania

Turtle Cake

1 pkg	German chocolate cake mix (1 lb, 2½ oz)
½ c	butter or margarine, softened
1½ c	water
½ c	oil
1 can	sweetened condensed milk (14 oz)
1 lb	caramels
	chopped pecans

Combine chocolate cake mix, butter, water, oil and half the condensed milk in mixing bowl; mix well. Pour half of the batter into a greased and floured 9 × 13 inch baking dish. Bake at 350° for 20 to 25 minutes. Melt and mix together caramels and remaining condensed milk over low heat until smooth. Spread over baked cake layer. Sprinkle generously with chopped nuts. Cover with remaining cake batter. Return to oven and bake 25 to 35 minutes longer or until cake tests done.

Frosting:

½ c	butter or margarine
3 T	cocoa powder
6 T	evaporated milk
1 pkg	powdered sugar (1 lb), sifted
1 T	vanilla

Combine butter, cocoa and evaporated milk in saucepan. Melt over low heat. Remove from heat and beat in powdered sugar and vanilla until smooth. Spread immediately.

Elaine Foster, San Mateo, California

Wine Cake

1 pkg	yellow cake mix
1 pkg	instant vanilla pudding
1 tsp	nutmeg
4	eggs
¾ c	cream sherry wine
¾ c	oil

Mix all ingredients. Bake in a Bundt pan for 1 hour at 350°.

Robin Westfield, Casper, Wyoming

Chocolate Kahlúa Cake

1 pkg	chocolate cake mix (no pudding)
1 pkg	chocolate instant pudding (3¾ oz)
1 pt	sour cream
4	eggs
¾ c	oil
⅓ c	Kahlúa
1 pkg	chocolate chips (6 oz)

Glaze:

1 c	powdered sugar, sifted
3 T	Kahlúa

Combine all ingredients except chocolate chips. Mix well. Now add chocolate chips and stir until mixed thoroughly. Pour into a greased Bundt pan. Bake at 350° for 1 hour or until tests done. To make glaze, mix sugar and Kahlúa together and drizzle over cake when cool.

Regina Freiberg, Newport Beach, California

Bunco Night JOURNAL

Date of Party

Hostess

Party Theme

Menu

Winners

Who Else Played

Memories of the Evening

Lemon Bread

This bread is so sweet and delicious, it can be served as a dessert.

⅓ c	melted butter (do not use margarine)
1 c	sugar
3 T	lemon extract
2	eggs
1½ c	sifted flour
1 tsp	baking powder
½ tsp	salt
½ c	milk
1½ T	grated lemon peel
½ c	chopped pecans
	Lemon Pour recipe (below)

Preheat oven to 350°. Grease and flour one 9 × 5 × 3 inch loaf pan. In a large bowl, mix butter, sugar and lemon extract; beat in eggs until creamy. In medium-sized bowl, sift together flour, baking powder and salt. Add flour mixture alternately with milk to butter mixture, stirring just enough to blend. Fold in lemon peel and pecans. Pour batter into pan. Bake 1 hour or until toothpick comes out clean. Cool in pan on rack 10 minutes.

Lemon Pour: In a small saucepan, stir ¼ cup lemon juice and ½ cup sugar together over medium heat until sugar is dissolved. Poke holes in top of loaf and drizzle Lemon Pour over top and into cracks. Let stand until glaze soaks into bread, about 5 minutes. Remove bread from pan. Wrap in foil. Let set at least 24 hours before slicing.

Donna Talbert, Fresno, California

Easy Cheesecake

Crust:

18	graham crackers
1 cube	butter

1–2 tsp cinnamon
⅓ c   sugar

Crush crackers and add remaining ingredients. Place in a 10-inch pie pan. Save 3 tablespoons of crust mixture for topping.

Filling:
12 oz   soft cream cheese
¾ c   sugar
2   eggs
2 tsp   vanilla

Mix all ingredients until smooth and pour into pie crust. Bake at 350° for 22 minutes.

Topping:
1 can   crushed pineapple (small), drained
1 ctn   sour cream (small)
⅓ c   sugar
1 tsp   vanilla

Mix well. Gently spoon topping over baked filling and bake 10 more minutes. Cool.

Georgia Santiago, Atlanta, Georgia

Easy Cream Cheese Clouds

1 pkg   cream cheese (8 oz)
½ c   powdered sugar
¼ tsp   vanilla extract
1 c   heavy cream
1 can   cherry pie filling
         chopped nuts (optional)

Mix cream cheese, sugar and vanilla at medium speed with electric mixer. Gradually add heavy cream, mix well. Whip until thickened. Using the back of a spoon, shape into 3½ inch shells. Place on waxed paper–lined cookie sheet. Freeze two hours or overnight. When ready to serve, fill with cherry pie filling. Sprinkle chopped nuts on top if desired. Yield: 10 servings.

Walter Thompson, Minneapolis, Minnesota

French Silk Chocolate Pie

1 c	butter or margarine
1½ c	sugar
4 oz	unsweetened chocolate, melted
2 tsp	vanilla
4	eggs
1	baked 9-inch pie shell, cooled
1	container whipped topping, small

In a small bowl, cream butter and sugar until light and fluffy. Add melted chocolate and vanilla and beat until smooth. Add 1 egg and beat for 5 minutes. Add 2 more eggs and beat 5 minutes again. Add remaining egg and beat 5 minutes more. Turn mixture into crust and chill 3 hours or until set. Spread with whipped topping.

Ginny White, Del Mar, California

Cherry Jell-O Dessert

1 c	sugar
¼ c	margarine, melted
1 c	walnuts, chopped
1 c	crushed pineapple, drained
2 bx	cherry Jell-O
24	graham crackers
	Cool Whip

Cream sugar and margarine. Add nuts and pineapple. Place 12 graham crackers on bottom of a 9 × 13 inch pan. Spread with pineapple and nut mixture. Place remaining crackers on top. Pour partially set Jell-O over crackers. Place in refrigerator until firm. Serve with Cool Whip.

Marci Davidson, Peoria, Illinois

Eggnog Pie

1 pkg	egg custard mix (4½ oz)
½ tsp	unflavored gelatin
½ c	milk
2 c	frozen whipped topping, thawed

¼ tsp   nutmeg
2 T   dark rum
1   baked 9-inch pie shell, cooled

Combine custard mix and gelatin in saucepan. Blend in milk. Bring to a boil, stirring constantly. Chill until thickened. Combine 1½ cups whipped topping, nutmeg and rum in a mixer bowl. Blend in custard mixture at low speed. Pour into pie shell. Chill until firm, about 3 hours. Garnish with remaining whipped topping and sprinkle with additional nutmeg and decorate with candies, if desired.

Regina Pendley, Newport Beach, California

Helen's Old-Fashioned Bread Pudding

This is a great recipe for any holiday gathering.
6   slices white bread, cubed
2 c   raisins (soaked in warm water for
         15 minutes)
4   eggs, beaten
2 tsp   cinnamon
scant c sugar
1 T   vanilla
1 qt   milk, scalded
¼ c   butter
         whipped topping (optional)

In a large mixing bowl, add bread and raisins. Meanwhile, in a separate bowl, beat eggs and add ½ of cinnamon, and the sugar and vanilla. Slowly pour scalded milk into egg mixture. Pour milk and egg mixture over bread and raisins and stir. Transfer mixture into greased 9 × 13 inch glass baking dish. Dot top with butter and rest of cinnamon. Set baking dish in pan of water and bake at 350° for about an hour. Stir mixture after 30 minutes, then continue baking. Serve warm with whipped topping. Yield: 8 to 10 servings.

Helen McPheeters, Newport Beach, California

**Bunco Night
JOURNAL**

Date of Party
_____

Hostess
_____

Party Theme
_____

Menu
_____
_____
_____
_____

Winners
_____
_____
_____
_____
_____

Who Else Played
_____
_____
_____
_____
_____

Memories
of the Evening
_____
_____
_____
_____
_____

Notes

Chocolate Fizz

2 pts chocolate ice cream
½ c hot fudge sauce (any jar variety is fine),
melted but not hot
soda water

Place two scoops of chocolate ice cream into 4 tall glasses. Pour 1 tablespoon hot fudge sauce into each glass. Fill the glasses with soda water and drizzle another tablespoon of fudge sauce over each. Yield: 4 drinks.

Denise Perchuck, Salt Lake City, Utah

Peach Ice Cream Soda

6 very ripe, fragrant peaches
½ c peach or apricot nectar
4 large scoops vanilla or peach ice cream
homemade soda water or plain seltzer
1 c heavy cream, whipped with 2 T sugar and
1 tsp vanilla extract

Peel and pit the peaches and slice into eighths. Distribute the slices evenly among 4 tall 12-ounce glasses. Add 2 T of the nectar to each glass and mash peaches lightly with a fork. Add 1 scoop of ice cream to each glass, add the soda water or seltzer, and stir lightly to mix. Top with a dollop of flavored whipped cream and serve. Yield: 4 drinks.

Denise Perchuck, Salt Lake City, Utah

Raspberry Surprise Bars

1 pkg butterscotch slice-and-bake cookies
8 oz cream cheese
2 T milk
½ c raspberry preserves

Slice cookies and place close together in a 9 × 13 inch cake pan. Bake 10 to 12 minutes, until golden brown. Mix cream cheese and milk together.

Spread cheese mixture on cookies immediately after removing from the oven. Spread preserves on top of cheese. Cool and cut into squares.

Jessica Lane, Yuma, Arizona

Candy

Mock Almond Roca

1 c	sweet butter
1 c	brown sugar
1 pkg	saltine crackers
3 c	chocolate chips (semisweet)
1–2 c	almonds, finely crushed

Melt butter and brown sugar in saucepan; let boil for 3 minutes. Line cookie sheet with foil and spray with nonstick cooking spray. Line pan with saltines, pour mixture over top and bake at 350° for 5 minutes. Cover with chocolate chips and spread when melted. Sprinkle almonds on top. Refrigerate until hard. Cut and serve.

Teri Allen, Irvine, California

Divinity Candy

2½ c	white sugar
½ c	white corn syrup
½ c	cold water
2	egg whites
1 c	nuts (if desired)
1 tsp	vanilla

Cook first 3 ingredients to 250°; pour over stiffly beaten egg whites. Cook rest of syrup to 263°; pour into egg mixture. Add vanilla. Beat until it starts to lose gloss; add nuts. Drop by teaspoonfuls onto waxed paper.

Katarina Buell, Jackson, Mississippi

See's Fudge

4 c	sugar
1 can	Pet milk (large)
½ lb	butter
3 pkgs	chocolate chips (6 oz)
24 lg	marshmallows
4 c	nutmeats (optional)
1 tsp	vanilla

Boil sugar and milk 10 minutes (no longer). Last 2 minutes, add butter. Remove from stove; add chocolate chips and stir. Add marshmallows and stir until melted. Add nuts and vanilla. Stir and pour into buttered 9 × 13 inch pan. Makes 5 pounds of delicious fudge.

Katarina Buell, Jackson, Mississippi

Million-Dollar Fudge

Prepare beforehand:

1 pkg	chocolate bits (12 oz)
1	plain Hershey's bar (10 oz)
1 pt	marshmallow cream
½ stk	butter
2 tsp	vanilla
	Add 1 cup chopped walnuts last

Cook:

| 4½ c | sugar |
| 1 can | condensed milk (large) |

Boil hard for 5 minutes. When done, stir in prepared ingredients until smooth.

Toni Bayuell, Lake Forest, California

Chocolate Fudge

Put in large bowl:

1½ c	chocolate chips
¼ lb	margarine
1 c	chopped nuts
1 tsp	vanilla

Melt in double boiler:

10 lg	marshmallows
1 tsp	water

Boil 6 minutes:

2 c	sugar
¾ c	evaporated milk

Pour hot mixes into chocolate and nut mixture. Mix, stir until melted and smooth. Put into greased pan. Chill.

Taylor Westin, Villa Park, California

Chocolate Candy Roll

2 sq	unsweetened chocolate
½ c	mayonnaise
1½ c	powdered sugar
1	egg, beaten
1 c	chopped nuts
1 pkg	small marshmallows (6½ oz)
1 pkg	coconut (3½ oz)

Melt chocolate and mayonnaise over low heat, stirring constantly. Cool slightly. Stir in powdered sugar and beaten egg. Cool. Fold in nuts and marshmallows. Stir until well coated. Shape soft candy into 2 rolls. Coat rolls with coconut. Wrap carefully. Store in freezer until needed. Cut into slices to serve.

Cameron Dawson, Vancouver, Washington

Bunco Night JOURNAL

Date of Party

Hostess

Party Theme

Menu

Winners

Who Else Played

Memories of the Evening

Nestlé Crunchy Fudge Sandwiches

1 pkg	Nestlé butterscotch chips (6 oz)
1/2 c	peanut butter
4 c	Rice Krispies
1 pkg	chocolate chips (6 oz)
1/2 c	sugar
2 T	butter (from measuring spoon, not wrapper)
1 T	water

Melt butterscotch chips and peanut butter in double boiler. Stir in cereal. Press 1/2 the mixture in an 8-inch buttered dish. Chill. Heat chocolate chips, sugar, butter and water in double boiler. Spread over cereal. Put remaining cereal on top. Press gently. Chill 1 hour. Yield: 25 (1 1/2 inch) squares.

Janis Haskin, Oakland, California

Peanut Brittle

1 c	water
1 c	white corn syrup
3 c	white sugar
1 pkg	raw Spanish peanuts
1 tsp	vanilla
2 T	butter
1 tsp	salt
1 T	soda

Cook water, syrup and sugar to 270°. Add raw peanuts and cook to 315°. Stir constantly so peanuts won't burn. Remove from heat and add vanilla and butter. Stir until butter is melted; add salt and soda. Stir briskly until peak of foaming is reached. Pour quickly into large, buttered pans; let cool. Break into pieces. Store in airtight containers in a cool, dry place.

Marcia Brook, Hartford, Connecticut

Sugar Nuts

1½ c	sugar
¼ c	honey
½ c	cold water
3 c	walnut halves
½ tsp	vanilla

Combine sugar, honey and water in a pan and cook until it reaches soft ball stage (238°). Remove from heat and add nuts and vanilla. Stir until syrup becomes creamy and thick. Turn onto waxed paper to harden, then break into pieces.

Judy Cannon, Green Bay, Wisconsin

Mint Puffs

Beat 3 egg whites to stiff peaks. Gradually add 1 cup sugar, beating after each addition. Add 1 cup mint chocolate chips. Add several drops green food coloring. Drop by spoonfuls on cookie sheet. Heat oven to 375° and turn off heat. Put puffs into oven and leave overnight.

Wendy Parsons, Gastonia, North Carolina

Caramel Corn

2 c	brown sugar
2 stk	butter or margarine
½ c	white corn syrup
1 tsp	salt
1 tsp	butter flavoring
½ tsp	burnt sugar flavoring
½ tsp	soda
16 c	popped corn

Combine brown sugar, butter, corn syrup and salt. Boil for 5 minutes. Remove from fire. Stir in flavorings and soda. Pour immediately over popcorn. Put in 1 or 2 large pans. Place in 250° oven for 1 hour, stirring about every 15 minutes. Cool. Keeps well in tight containers.

Nancy Donner, Birmingham, Alabama

Temperature Tests for Candy Making

Two methods of determining when candy has been cooked to the proper consistency is by using a candy thermometer in order to record degrees or by using the cold water test. Use the chart below to help follow candy recipes:

Type of Candy	Degrees	Cold Water
Fondant, Fudge	234–238°	Soft Ball
Divinity, Caramels	245–248°	Firm Ball
Taffy	265–270°	Hard Ball
Butterscotch	275–289°	Light Crack
Peanut Brittle	285–290°	Hard Crack
Caramelized Sugar	310–321°	Caramelized

In using the Cold Water Test, use a fresh cupful of cold water for each test. When testing, remove the candy from the fire and pour about ½ teaspoon of candy into the cold water. Pick the candy up in the fingers and roll into a ball if possible.

In the Soft Ball Test the candy will roll into a soft ball that quickly loses its shape when removed from the water.

In the Firm Ball Test the candy will roll into a firm but not hard ball. It will flatten out a few minutes after being removed from water.

In the Hard Ball Test the candy will roll into a hard ball that has lost almost all plasticity and will roll around on a plate on removal from the water.

In the Light Crack Test the candy will form brittle threads that will soften on removal from the water.

In the Hard Crack Test the candy will form brittle threads in the water that will remain brittle after being removed from the water.

In Caramelizing, the sugar first melts, then becomes a golden brown. It will form a hard brittle ball in cold water.

Quick Meals for a Quick Bunco Getaway

**Don't Be Late to Bunco
Because You Have to
Get the Family Fed—
Use These Quick, Easy Meal
Ideas
Even the Kids Can
Help Prepare**

Notes

*G*etting out of the house on Bunco night can sometimes be difficult with a family to feed. The following section was designed to help moms prepare quick meals that are sure to please the whole family.

Many of the recipes included here are one-dish meals to save you time. We have also provided meal ideas that you can complete simply by adding a green salad with one of our delicious dressings, fresh, steamed vegetables (frozen vegetables work great too!) or fresh fruit. Who said good, nutritious meals can't be simple?

Mini Pizza

Serve with a green salad.

6	English muffins
1 jar	spaghetti sauce or pizza sauce
1 c	mozzarella cheese, shredded pepperoni

*S*pread sauce over muffins. Top with cheese and pepperoni. Bake at 400° until cheese melts.

Pizza Bread

Serve with cold, fresh carrots, broccoli, celery and cauliflower, and creamy Italian dressing for dipping.

1	loaf French bread, sliced in half lengthwise
¼ c	butter or margarine, softened
1	garlic clove, minced
1 can	tomato sauce (7½ oz)
2 T	tomato paste
1 tsp	dried basil
1 tsp	dried oregano
½ lb	pepperoni
2½ c	mozzarella cheese, shredded
¾ c	Parmesan cheese, shredded

Mix butter with garlic and spread over loaf halves. Mix together tomato sauce, tomato paste, basil and oregano. Spread over buttered bread. Add pepperoni and cheeses. Place loaves on cookie sheet. Bake at 400° for 10 to 12 minutes or until cheese melts. Slice and serve with Caesar salad (page 52).

Sharon Carpenter, Norwalk, California

Pizza Cups

Serve with a green or Jell-O fruit salad.

¾ lb	ground beef
1 can	tomato paste (6 oz)
1 T	minced onions
1 tsp	Italian seasoning
1 tsp	basil
½ tsp	salt/pepper
	parsley
	chili powder
	garlic
1 can	refrigerator biscuits (10 oz)
¾ c	mozzarella cheese, shredded

Brown and drain beef. Stir in tomato paste, onion and seasonings. Cook over low heat 5 minutes, stirring frequently. Place biscuits in greased muffin tins, pressing to cover bottom and sides. Spoon ¼ cup mixture into biscuits and sprinkle with cheese. Bake at 400° for 12 minutes. Yield: 10 to 12 cups.

Denise Riches, Irvine, California

Lasagna Roll-Ups

Serve with cool, parboiled vegetables marinated in Italian dressing and garlic bread.

1 c	ricotta cheese
1 c	mozzarella cheese, shredded
1	egg
1 pkg	frozen spinach (10 oz), chopped, cooked and drained
½ tsp	oregano
1 tsp	salt
1	recipe spaghetti sauce (jar or homemade)

Cook six to eight lasagna noodles according to package directions. Meanwhile, mix everything together except the sauce. Add ½ cup cheese mixture to one end of noodle and roll up. Cover with sauce. Sprinkle with mozzarella cheese. Cover and bake at 350° for 35 minutes or until heated through. Yield: 6 servings.

Cathy Yeager, Montreal, Canada

Cheese and Hot Dog Crescents

Serve with a fresh fruit salad.

8	hot dogs
4	American cheese slices, each cut into 6 strips
1 tube	crescent-style dinner rolls (8 oz)

Make a slit in each hot dog and put 3 strips of cheese inside slits. Separate dough into 8 triangles, wrap dough around dogs. Keep cheese side up. Place on cookie sheet and bake at 375° for 12 to 15 minutes.

Toni Fauster, Lake Forest, California

Oriental Pepper Steak and Rice

Have all the ingredients ready before you start stir-frying this super-fast steak. Serve with white rice and steamed oriental vegetables.

2 T	margarine
8	scallions, cut into ¼-inch pieces
1	medium bell pepper, cut into strips
1	round steak, cut into 2-inch strips, marinated in ¼ cup soy sauce
1 T	cornstarch
1 c	soy sauce
1 c	bean sprouts
1 can	water chestnuts, drained and quartered
6	cherry tomatoes, cut in half
2 c	cooked rice
1 c	sweet and sour sauce

Melt margarine in a large skillet and sauté scallions and bell pepper until tender, about 2 minutes. Stir in steak and the marinade. Cook until meat is done. Combine cornstarch with soy sauce. Pour liquid mixture into skillet and stir constantly until mixture thickens. Add bean sprouts and water chestnuts. Simmer 5 minutes. Just before serving, gently stir in cherry tomato halves. Serve on a bed of rice and garnish with additional bean sprouts, if desired. Serve sweet and sour sauce on the side. Yield: 4 generous servings.

Alice Park, Polk City, Florida

Bunco Night JOURNAL

Date of Party

Hostess

Party Theme

Menu

Winners

Who Else Played

Memories
of the Evening

Slow-Cooked Flank Steak and Teriyaki Potatoes

Steak:

1	flank steak (about 1½ lb), cut in half
1 T	vegetable oil
1	large onion, sliced
⅓ c	water
1 can	chopped green chilies (4 oz)
2 T	vinegar
1 tsp	chili powder
1 tsp	garlic powder
½ tsp	sugar
½ tsp	salt
⅛ tsp	pepper

In a skillet, brown steak in oil; transfer to a slow cooker. In the same skillet, sauté onion for 1 minute. Gradually add water, stirring to loosen browned bits from pan. Add remaining ingredients; bring to a boil. Pour over the flank steak. Cover and cook on low for 7 to 8 hours or until the meat is tender. Slice and serve with gravy.

Gail Keyport, Littleton, Colorado

Potatoes:

1½ lb	new potatoes
1 T	butter, cut into pieces
1 T	teriyaki sauce
¼ tsp	garlic salt
¼ tsp	Italian seasoning
	dash of black pepper
	dash of ground red pepper

Wash and scrub potatoes. Cut into 1-inch pieces. Place potatoes in 1½-quart microwave casserole dish. Add butter, teriyaki, garlic salt, Italian seasoning and peppers. Toss; cover; microwave on 100% power 12 to 15 minutes. Stir twice while cooking. Yield: 5 servings.

Debra Thomas, Medford, Oregon

Salisbury Steak and Easy Sliced Potatoes

Steak:

1 c	cream of mushroom soup
1 lb	ground beef
1/3 c	fine, dry bread crumbs
1/2 c	finely chopped onion
1	large egg, beaten

Combine 1/4 cup soup and remaining ingredients in a large bowl; stir well. Shape mixture into six patties. Brown patties in a large skillet over medium heat. Remove patties. Combine remaining soup and add some water to make gravy. Return patties to pan and simmer 20 to 30 minutes. Yield: 4 servings.

Vera Riches, Thousand Oaks, California

Potatoes:

These potatoes also make a great side dish to meatloaf.

	potatoes, any variety, enough to fill the dish you're using
	salt and pepper
4 T	butter, melted

Wash, but do not peel potatoes. Slice into 1/4-inch slices and layer in a well-buttered casserole dish. Sprinkle salt and pepper on each layer. Pour melted butter over potatoes. Cover and bake at 375° for 45 minutes or until potatoes are tender when a fork is inserted.

Kim Smith, Oceanside, California

Bunco Night JOURNAL

Date of Party

Hostess

Party Theme

Menu

Winners

Who Else Played

Memories of the Evening

Stuffed Baked Potatoes

This can be served as an appetizer or an entrée accompanied by a green salad and vegetables.

4 lg	Idaho potatoes
1 lb	ground beef, cooked and drained
½ c	butter
½ c	cooked mushrooms
5 T	sour cream
3	scallions, chopped
1 tsp	seasoning salt
½ tsp	pepper
4	slices American cheese
5	slices bacon, cooked, drained, crumbled

Wash potatoes and bake in foil. Open gently and carefully split down middle; scoop out all meat of potato into a large mixing bowl. Add rest of ingredients except bacon and cheese. Mix well. Stuff potato skins with potato mixture; top with cheese and bacon. Pop back into oven and heat until cheese melts. Yield: 4 servings.

Linda Devon, Huntsville, Alabama

Chili Spaghetti

Serve with a salad and Mozzarella Toast (page 41).

1 lb	ground beef
½ c	onion, chopped
2	garlic cloves, minced
3 c	tomato juice
1 can	kidney beans (16 oz), rinsed and drained
6 oz	spaghetti, broken into 3-inch pieces
1 T	Worcestershire sauce
1 tsp	chili powder
1 tsp	salt
½ tsp	pepper

In a skillet over medium heat, cook beef, onion and garlic until meat is no longer pink; drain.

Transfer to a greased 2½-quart baking dish; stir in remaining ingredients. Cover and bake at 350° for 65 to 70 minutes or until spaghetti is just tender. Let stand, covered, for 10 minutes before serving. Yield: 6 servings.

Annabelle Kinsky, Lake Arrowhead, California

Parmesan Chicken Fingers and Parmesan Potato Rounds

Chicken:

4	boneless, skinless chicken breasts
⅓ c	bread crumbs (Italian style)
⅓ c	Parmesan cheese, shredded
½ tsp	paprika
1	egg, lightly beaten
2 T	butter, melted
	salt and pepper
1	clove garlic, minced

Cut chicken into ½-inch-wide strips. Mix together bread crumbs, Parmesan cheese, and paprika. Dip each strip into egg and then into bread crumbs. Place chicken on a cookie sheet. Mix together butter, salt, pepper and garlic, drizzle over chicken. Bake at 450° for 6 minutes per side or until cooked through.

Amy Buckwald, Tulsa, Oklahoma

Potatoes:

4	medium red potatoes, thinly sliced
1	small onion, finely chopped
3 T	melted butter
¼ c	Parmesan cheese, shredded
¼ tsp	salt
⅛ tsp	pepper
⅛ tsp	garlic powder

Layer potatoes and onions in a greased baking dish. Put remaining ingredients on top. Bake, uncovered, at 450° for 25 to 30 minutes or until tender. Yield: 4 servings.

Patty Ulrich, St. George, Utah

Crusty Baked Chicken and Cheddar Baked Potato Slices

Chicken:

6	chicken breasts, boneless and skinless
1	egg
¼ c	milk
1 c	instant potato flakes
1 tsp	paprika
1 tsp	garlic salt
½ c	Parmesan cheese, shredded
2 T	melted butter

Wash chicken. In a bowl, beat egg and milk. In a separate bowl, combine potato flakes, paprika, garlic salt and cheese. Dip chicken into egg mixture, then roll in potato mixture to coat evenly. Place in a greased baking dish. Drizzle with melted butter. Bake at 400° for 35 minutes. Turn chicken and increase temperature to 425°, bake 10 to 15 minutes longer. Yield: 6 servings.

DeAnna McKelvie, Huntington Beach, California

Potatoes:

1 can	cream of mushroom soup
½ tsp	paprika
½ tsp	pepper
4	medium potatoes, sliced ¼-inch thick
1 c	Cheddar cheese, shredded

Combine soup, paprika, and pepper. In a greased baking dish, arrange potato slices in overlapping rows. Sprinkle with cheese and then spoon mixture over potatoes. Cover with foil. Bake at 400° for 45 minutes. Yield: 6 servings.

Karen Foust, Spokane, Washington

Dijon Chicken and Rice

4	boneless chicken breasts
1 tsp	onion salt
½ tsp	lemon pepper
1 pkg	regular long grain and wild rice (6 oz) or 2 cups hot cooked white rice
3 T	butter or margarine
1 c	chicken broth
½ c	light cream
2 T	flour
1 T	Dijon mustard

Sprinkle chicken with onion salt and lemon pepper. Prepare rice. Meanwhile, in a skillet over medium heat, cook chicken in butter or margarine about 20 minutes or until tender. Remove to a platter and keep warm. Add chicken broth to pan. Stir together cream and flour; add to broth. Cook and stir until thickened and bubbly. Cook and stir 1 to 2 minutes more. Stir in mustard. To serve, spoon sauce over chicken and rice. Yield: 4 servings.

Samantha Crone, Idaho Falls, Idaho

Chicken Tomato Vinaigrette and Parmesan Rotini

Chicken:

2 T	olive oil, divided
1	garlic clove, minced
⅛ tsp	crushed red pepper
¼ tsp	dried basil
1	3-inch strip lemon peel
1 can	tomatoes, cut up and drained
½ tsp	sugar
1 T	wine vinegar
¼ tsp	salt
2 T	parsley, chopped and divided
4	chicken breasts
1 T	butter or margarine

Bunco Night JOURNAL

Date of Party
_____

Hostess
_____

Party Theme
_____

Menu
_____
_____
_____
_____

Winners
_____
_____
_____
_____
_____

Who Else Played
_____
_____
_____
_____
_____

Memories of the Evening
_____
_____
_____
_____

Notes

In a skillet, heat 1 tablespoon olive oil over medium heat. Add garlic, red pepper and basil; cook 1 minute. Add lemon peel, tomatoes and sugar, breaking up tomatoes into small chunks. Simmer 20 minutes. Remove from heat; stir in vinegar, salt and 1 tablespoon parsley. Remove lemon peel; set aside. While sauce cooks, place chicken between 2 sheets of waxed paper; pound to ¼-inch to ½-inch thickness. In a large skillet, heat remaining oil with butter or margarine over medium-high heat. Add chicken. Cook about 3 minutes on each side; remove and keep warm. Add tomato sauce to skillet; heat 1 minute, stirring constantly. Pour over chicken; sprinkle with remaining parsley. Yield: 4 servings.

Patty Bandos, Temecula, California

Pasta:

½ lb	rotini pasta
2 T	butter, softened
⅓ c	Parmesan cheese, shredded
2 T	sour cream
	salt and pepper

Cook rotini according to package directions. Drain well. Toss rotini with butter, cheese, and sour cream. Add salt and pepper to taste. Yield: 4 servings.

Susan Kamstra, Westlake Village, California

Chicken and Sausage Cassoulet

3	medium carrots, cut into ½-inch pieces
1	medium onion, chopped
⅓ c	water
1 can	tomato paste (6 oz)
½ c	dry red wine or cooking sherry
1 tsp	garlic powder
2	bay leaves
½ tsp	dried thyme, crushed
2 cans	navy beans (15 oz), drained

| 3 | boneless, skinless chicken breasts, shredded or cut into bite-size pieces |
| ½ lb | fully cooked Polish sausage, sliced ¼-inch thick |

In a small saucepan, combine carrots, onion and water; bring to a boil; reduce heat. Simmer covered 5 minutes. Transfer to a slow cooker. Stir in tomato paste, wine and seasonings. Add beans, chicken and sausage. Cover; cook on low heat for 6 hours. Remove bay leaves and skim fat. Yield: 4 servings.

Emily Zacaro, San Diego, California

Turkey Enchilada Pie

This is a great use for leftover turkey or chicken. Combine this tasty pie with a vegetable-packed salad and one of our delicious salad dressings, and you're done!

1	onion, finely chopped
1 T	oil
1 can	diced green chilies
2 c	turkey or chicken, cooked and cubed
4	flour tortillas (8-inch)
1 can	La Victoria Enchilada Sauce (mild)
	Jack cheese, shredded
	Cheddar cheese, shredded

Cook onion in oil until tender. Add green chilies and turkey or chicken; cook 5 minutes; set aside. In a skillet with hot oil, cook flour tortillas about 5 seconds on each side to soften. In the bottom of a 9-inch round pan, spread a little enchilada sauce, add one flour tortilla, then spread turkey mixture over, then a portion of the enchilada sauce, then spread cheeses and top with another flour tortilla; repeat 2 more times. Top with last four tortillas, remainder of enchilada sauce and cheeses. Bake covered with foil at 350° for 20 minutes; remove foil and bake another 15 minutes. Yield: 4 to 6 servings.

Denise Riches, Irvine, California

Pork Chop and Rice Bake

Top off this easy meal with a fresh fruit salad.

¾ c	raw rice
4–6	pork chops
1 can	beef consommé soup
½ c	water
1	onion, sliced
½	green pepper, sliced
¼ tsp	marjoram
¼ tsp	thyme
	salt and pepper

Spray a 9 × 13 inch baking dish with nonstick cooking spray. Pour raw rice in pan and place pork chops on top. Pour soup and water over top. Place onion and green pepper slices evenly over top. Sprinkle with seasonings. Bake, covered with foil, at 350° for 1 hour; remove foil and cook an additional 15 minutes or until liquid is absorbed.

Donna Thomas, Fremont, California

Ham and Noodles

This recipe also makes a great Bunco entrée. Serve with vegetable soup or green salad.

8 oz	egg noodles
8 T	butter
¼ c	onion, finely chopped
½ c	sour cream
3	eggs, lightly beaten
1 c	ham, cooked and diced
	fresh-ground black pepper
	salt
¼ c	bread crumbs

Preheat oven to 350°. Cook noodles until barely tender; rinse and drain. Melt half the butter in an 8-inch skillet. Add onions and cook 4 to 5 minutes until translucent. Add noodles and remaining butter; toss to coat noodles well. With a whisk, beat sour cream and eggs in a large bowl. Stir in ham, a generous grinding of pepper, salt and contents of skillet. Butter a 2-quart casserole dish; add bread crumbs to coat bottom and sides evenly. Fill casserole with noodle and ham mixture. Bake, uncovered, for 45 minutes or until mixture is firm. This can be served right out of the casserole dish or turned onto a warmed platter. Yield: 4 servings.

Jacqueline Eller, Chicago, Illinois

Pork Chops Abracadabra

For a complete meal, add vegetables under the chops halfway through cooking. Serve chops and gravy over white rice.

4–6   pork chops
         salt and pepper to taste

One of the following:
         cream of mushroom soup
         cream of chicken soup
         sweet and sour sauce
         chicken and rice soup
         barbecue sauce

Season both sides of pork chops with salt and pepper. Place in slow cooker. Pour one of the sauces over the top of the chops. Cook 6 to 8 hours on low.

Mary Chambers, Las Vegas, Nevada

Chicken-Fried Chops

This slow-cooked meal is effortless! Serve chops and gravy over rice and add your favorite fresh vegetables.

½ c   flour
2 tsp   salt
1 tsp   mustard
½ tsp   garlic powder
4–6   pork chops, fat trimmed

Bunco Night JOURNAL

Date of Party

Hostess

Party Theme

Menu

Winners

Who Else Played

Memories of the Evening

2 T   vegetable oil
1 can   cream of chicken soup
⅓ c   water

In a bowl, combine flour, salt, mustard and garlic powder; dip chops in mixture. Quickly brown the chops in a skillet with oil. Place in a slow cooker. Combine soup and water; pour over chops. Cover and cook on low for 6 to 8 hours or until meat is tender. Yield: 4 to 6 servings.

Vivian Gerber, Cleveland, Ohio

Skillet Kielbasa Meal

This quick one-dish meal is sure to please.

1 can   cream of celery soup
¾ c   water
1 T   butter or margarine
1 lb   smoked kielbasa, cut into bite-size
         pieces
¾ c   uncooked long grain rice
1 pkg   frozen peas (10 oz)
1 jar   sliced mushrooms (4½ oz), drained
1 c   Cheddar cheese, shredded

In a skillet, combine soup, water and butter; bring to a boil. Add kielbasa and rice. Reduce heat; cover and simmer for 20 minutes or until rice is tender. Stir in peas and mushrooms. Cover and simmer 15 more minutes. Sprinkle with cheese; cover and let stand until cheese is melted. Yield: 4 to 6 servings.

Faith Harper, Phoenix, Arizona

Bunco
the Game

Includes:
- **Bunco Origin and History**
- **The World Bunco Association™**
- **Official Bunco Rules**
- **Theme Party Ideas**
- **Bunco Night Journal**

Bunco Origin and History

This progressive dice game, under its original name of 8-Dice Cloth, was played in England during the eighteenth century. It was unknown in the United States until 1855, when it was introduced into San Francisco during the Gold Rush by a crooked gambler. This shady character, traveling from the East to West Coast, had made many stops en route to the California goldfields. He also made various changes to the gambling game he called Banco.

After a few years the game and activity was re-christened Bunco or Bunko. During this same period, a Spanish card game, Banca, and its Mexican derivative, Monte, were also introduced to the population of San Francisco.

Bunco Dice and Bunco Cards were combined to form a more efficient method of separating the hardworking citizens from their money at numerous gambling locations. These locations were known as Bunco parlors. Hence, the word Bunco came to be a general term that applied to all schemes, swindling and confidence games. After the Civil War and into the turn of the century, Bunco flourished as the population grew and the economy recovered. Between 1870 and 1880 in virtually every large city in the country, Bunco-Banco games were in operation. Some Bunco locations were furnished elaborately while others resembled professional offices. During the 1880s and into the mid-1890s, Bunco was played in Texas and Oklahoma, through Kansas and Missouri, in towns and cities along the Ohio and Mississippi Rivers, and from New York to the Great Lake states.

Through the Victorian era and prior to WWI, Bunco had achieved permanent placement as a traditional family or parlor game, promoting social interaction. During this period, Bunco groups consisting of 8 to 12 people and as many as 20 people enjoyed an evening of food, drink, conversation and friendly competition.

During Prohibition and the Roaring '20s, the infamous Bunco gambling parlors re-surfaced in various regions of the U.S. The most notorious speakeasies and Bunco dice parlors were located in and around Chicago, Illinois. The term "Bunco Squad" referred to the detectives who raided these establishments.

After Prohibition, Bunco group activity declined in the major cities of the country, but spread to the suburbs as housing development and the migratory population expanded nationally. Not much was heard about Bunco activity from 1940 to 1980 (WWII, Korea, Vietnam). Since the early 1980s, Bunco group activity has increased due to a combination of circumstances: a return to traditional family values, a sense of neighborhood and community, and the desire and need for social interaction. Most Bunco groups consist of 12 players (usually groups of women and occasionally couples). Kids are even beginning to play at parties and other social events. Playing Bunco is a great way to maintain relationships and make new friends. Bunco is a game of dice, luck and prizes.

The World Bunco Association™

The World Bunco Association was chartered in 1996, and is dedicated to the organization, preservation, promotion and the expansion of Bunco group activity.

The WBA is the official source and sanctioning body of Bunco games, products, a quarterly newsletter and accessories.

The World Bunco Association invites you to visit us on the Internet at **www.worldbunco.com** to find the latest in Bunco news and products, including newsletter subscriptions, additional copies of the cookbook and Bunco accessories. You can also register in our guest book, send us personal e-mail messages and look for new and exciting Bunco information. Let us know what you think of the site . . . we appreciate your comments. We would also like feedback about your Bunco playing experiences, rituals and game rules so we can share your ideas with other enthusiastic Bunco players.

Official BUNCO Rules

©1996, 2003 World Bunco Association

OBJECT OF THE GAME
The object of a Bunco is to roll the dice and accumulate the most "Wins" or "Buncos" during 4 sets of play.

WHAT YOU'LL NEED FOR 12 PLAYERS
1 set of Official Bunco Rules, 12 score sheets, 6 tally sheets, 9 dice, 1 bell, 6 pencils, 1 fuzzy die

SETUP FOR 12 PLAYERS
You will need 3 tables with 4 chairs at each table. Supply each table with 3 dice, 2 pencils and 2 tally sheets. Place the bell and fuzzy die at the head table.

Take the 12 score sheets and secretly draw a star on the back of four sheets. Have each person pick a score sheet; this will tell you who will be starting at the head table. The remaining 8 players can sit at Table 2 or Table 3.

Each table is randomly divided into 2 teams. Team couples sit across from each other. Pick one person on each team to tally points during each round.

DEFINITIONS

BUNCO ....Rolling three of a kind of the same number of the round you're on is a Bunco. For example, rolling three "fours" in Round 4 or three "sixes" in Round 6 is a Bunco. The player must call out "Bunco" to receive 21 points for the temporary team score on the tally sheet. <u>IMPORTANT: **Only the player who rolls the Bunco gets one Bunco point on her individual score sheet.**</u> Rolling three of a kind other than the number of the round you're on is worth five points for the temporary team score on the tally sheet. For example, rolling three "sixes" in Round 4 is worth five points. A player continues rolling until no points are rolled.

ROUND ....A round is a full turn of the number currently being rolled. As noted on the score sheet, each set is broken down into 6 rounds.
SET ....The game is divided into 4 sets. One set equals 6 rounds.
DIE ....Singular for Dice. When a player rolls a Bunco, she keeps the fuzzy die until the next Bunco is rolled.
HEAD TABLE ....The head table controls the pace of the game.
GHOST ....If there are not enough players, a ghost player can be substituted. The ghost moves from chair to chair like any player would. If the ghost rolls a Bunco, her team gets the 21 points and her teammate gets the Bunco point.
ROLL-OFF ....If the score is tied at the end of a round, there is a "Roll-Off." A Roll-Off is one complete turn around the table—rolling the current number "up"—playing one full round at the table while collecting points. The team with the most points after the Roll-Off is the winner and moves up a table.

HOW TO PLAY FOR 12 PLAYERS

The head table controls the pace of the game. The game begins when the head table rings the bell. One player from each table starts the game by trying to roll "ones" with the 3 dice. Always take your roll using 3 dice. If one of the dice shows the number currently "up," tally 1 point. If two of the dice show the number currently "up," tally 2 points.

When one team at the head table scores 21 points, or gets a Bunco, the scorekeeper rings the bell, which signals the end of the round for ALL tables. Players at the secondary tables who are in the middle of their turn may finish their turn and add those points to their score. The team with the highest score at each table at that time wins the round. (Remember, all players continue to roll and score until the bell is rung, even if their team has already reached 21 points.)

Rolling three of a kind of the same number of the round you're on is a Bunco. For example, rolling three "fours" in Round 4 or three "sixes" in Round 6 is a Bunco. The player must call out "Bunco" to receive 21 points for the temporary team score on the tally sheet. **IMPORTANT: Only the player who rolls the Bunco gets one Bunco point on her individual score sheet.**

Rolling three of a kind other than the number of the round you're on is worth five points for the temporary team score on the tally sheet. For example, rolling three "sixes" in Round 4 is worth five points. A player continues rolling until no points are rolled.

EXAMPLE: <u>Round 1</u>
(Each "one" rolled is worth one point.)
<u>Player rolls:</u>

-two "ones" are rolled. Player has 2 points and rolls all 3 dice again.

-a "one" is rolled. Player now has 3 points (2 and 1), and rolls all 3 dice again.

-no points are rolled. The dice are passed clockwise to the next player. The team scorekeeper writes down 3 points on the team tally sheet.

<u>If a player rolls:</u>

-Bunco! Three of a kind of the number of the present round (three "ones" in Round 1). A Bunco is worth 21 points for the team score on the tally sheet. Remember: Only the player who rolls the Bunco gets one Bunco point on her score sheet.

<u>If a player rolls:</u>

-three of a kind (but not Bunco), scores 5 points. Player rolls all 3 dice again. The team scorekeeper adds 5 points to the score on their tally sheet.

AT THE END OF EACH ROUND
When a team at the head table reaches 21 points or rolls a Bunco, they ring the bell to signal the end of the round. Each player marks a "W" (win) or "L" (loss) in the space provided for the first round on their individual score sheet. This is determined by the team with the highest score. In case of a tie, see ROLL-OFF section.

The winning team stays at the head table. Have one teammate move over a chair so she will have different partners for the next round. The losing team from the head table goes down to Table 2. The winning team from Table 2 goes to the head table and the winning team from Table 3 goes to Table 2. The losing team from Table 2 goes to Table 3 and the losing team from Table 3 stays at their table but one player moves over one chair so she will have a different partner.

The head table rings the bell to signal the start of Round 2. Each player rolls for "twos" in the second round. Play continues for 2 complete sets (6 rounds per set). At this point, take a break for dessert and continue the last 2 sets. The game ends when all 4 sets of Bunco have been completed. Each person then adds up her total Buncos, wins and losses from each round and writes the totals at the bottom of her score sheet. Prizes are awarded at this time.

PRIZE SELECTION FOR ADULT BUNCO PARTIES

<u>The prize values equal the suggested $5 contribution made by each player at the beginning of the game.</u> The prizes (gifts or cash) are selected by the host prior to the game with the above contribution. The winners are determined at the end of the game after each player totals up their Buncos, wins and losses for each round. Each player writes her total at the bottom of her score sheet. The host for the party then awards the prizes. If there is a tie score for a particular prize, there is a ROLL-OFF and the highest roll receives the prize.

$20 Prize = Most BUNCOS ~ for the player that rolls the most BUNCOS.

$15 Prize = Most WINS ~ for the player with the most WINS.

$10 Prize = Traveling ~ for the player who rolled the last BUNCO and is holding the fuzzy die at the end.

$8 Prize = 50/50 ~ for the player with equal WINS and LOSSES.

$5 Prize = Most LOSSES ~ for the player with the most LOSSES.

$2 Prize = "At Least I'm Taking Something Home Prize" ~ collect the remaining score sheets from players without prizes and the host draws a winner.

STARTING A BUNCO CLUB

Get 12 people together who want to meet once a month or once a week. Pick a month or week that each person will be host. Once established, it helps to give each member a copy of the Bunco party dates. If a member can't make a party, just call another friend or have a list of alternates available or substitute a ghost. A ghost is a player that travels from table to table like a regular player would. Have the ghost's partner for each round roll both turns.

ORGANIZING A BUNCO PARTY

Arrange to serve appetizers and dinner before the playing starts. Some hosts have a potluck party. Others prefer to have each host supply food and drinks. Go ahead and dine at the Bunco-playing tables.

After dinner is served, pass out the score sheets to determine who will play at the head table. See SETUP section.

After the first two complete sets, players take a break and dessert is served. Have players put their own score sheets at the appropriate head table, Table 2 or Table 3 for the second half of the game.

When the game is completed and scores tallied, prizes are then awarded.

CAN WE PLAY WITH MORE OR LESS THAN 12 PLAYERS?

Yes. Simply increase or reduce the number of tables per number of players (4 players per table). You must of course obtain three additional dice for each additional table. Using a ghost as described above can accommodate an odd number of players.

Theme Party Ideas

Bunco parties with a different theme each month are a fun way to add a little variety to your Bunco evenings. Below we've given you some ideas for themes you can use, but don't stop there. Use your creativity to come up with theme party ideas of your own.

The hostess creates her own theme idea and can start the ball rolling by sending out invitations ahead of time announcing the theme for the evening (allow extra planning time if players are responsible for bringing or making something). "Dress" the house to create a festive atmosphere. Have something fun for each player to wear when she arrives to get into the spirit. The food you serve should also coordinate with your theme if possible, and prizes (a must for theme parties) can also reflect the theme of the evening.

Theme parties are loads of fun to create and attend. We'd like to hear about your favorite theme parties so we can share them with other Bunco players.

'60s Theme Party

Throwing a '60s theme Bunco party is always fun. Send invitations that are "cut-out" flowers. Write "BUNCO POWER" on the front with all the other information inside. Ask everyone to dress with the sixties in mind: tie-dyed shirts, old bell-bottoms, beads, etc. Give a sixties-related theme prize for the best outfit: a sixties tape or CD, even candles make great gifts for this party. Play sixties music throughout the night to add to your theme atmosphere.

"Come as You Are" Bunco Party

Everyone gets a big kick out of this themed party. Send invitations as you would for your basic Bunco party. After the invitations are received, call all your guests at a time when you think they might be wearing some attire they would prefer not to be seen in. Ask them what they are wearing when you call and tell them your theme for the upcoming Bunco night is a "COME AS YOU ARE PARTY"!!! They must come in whatever they are wearing at the time you call. You'll all have lots of laughs and fun with this and it makes for great conversation at the party.

Hawaiian Theme

This is a good spring or summer theme to use. Have your guests dress with a Hawaiian flair. Aloha-printed dresses or skirts, even grass skirts with bathing suit tops (for the daring), help to make the evening festive. Tiki torch lights lining the driveway or in the yard set the tone for a fun Hawaiian theme. If it's warm enough, you can even have your party in a backyard setting. Serve "Pou Pous" (Hawaiian for appetizer) instead of a full-course meal. Prepare a basket with leis for your group; everyone picks one on entering. Have four of them secretly marked. These four designate who gets to start at the head table. Make a flowered headdress lei. Whoever rolls the Bunco wears the lei. The player wearing the lei at the end of the evening takes it home with a special prize.

Here Comes the Bunco Bride

This is always a favorite with Bunco players. Have all your gals wear their old wedding dresses (bridesmaid dresses will also do). Everyone gets a good laugh from this one. Some of the dresses will still fit . . . others will not. Some will come with dresses pinned, others partially zipped or buttoned. Possibly the dresses shrank . . . or maybe the gals have changed a size or two!! You can create a funny veil to be worn and passed from player to player as Buncos are being rolled. This is great fun. Take lots of photos . . . you probably won't get them in those dresses again.

Mexican Theme Party

This is also great for a Cinco de Mayo celebration. All your food dishes should be Mexican, of course. Prior to this evening, ask all your guests to decorate a sombrero of their own to be worn to the party. Give a prize at the end of the night for the most original. Decorate with the Mexican colors in mind. Use red, green and white to decorate your tables. Balloons always add a nice touch and make the room look festive. Send invitations with the Mexican flag printed on them. Use sombreros turned upside down to hold your appetizers, chips and salsa, etc. "Ceviche" is a great starter and can be made ahead of time. Our "Green Chili Bites" are also a good appetizer for this evening, or the "Gazpacho Soup." Add the "Chicken Tortilla Casserole" and you have a complete meal. To top off the evening, prepare our "Chocolate Kahlúa Cake." It's easy to make and can be made a day ahead of time. Everyone will want this recipe.

Pajama Bunco Party

Terrific fun will be had by all at this theme party. Have everyone wear their pajamas or pajamas and bathrobes and slippers. There are even chenille Bunco bathrobes with big dice on them, and they have "BUNCO" written down the front of the robe. They are adorable. Serve a brunch-type menu, perhaps our "Potato Quiche" with fresh fruit and "Monkey Bread." This will be a party to remember and everyone will already be dressed for bed when they get home.

St. Patrick's Day Bunco

Send cut-out shamrocks for invitations, adding "Mc" or "O" to their last name and ask all your players to dress in green attire. Serve our "Irish Stew" or the "Corned Beef Dinner" or perhaps an assortment of corned beef sandwiches. Irish beer, with a tint of green food coloring, or green-dyed punch is a must. For table snacks, gold chocolate coins, pistachios and assorted green candies such as jelly beans add a great touch. The "Luck of the Irish" is sure to be with you this night.

Valentine's Day Bunco Party

For your February Bunco Party, consider hosting a Valentine's Day party. Send Bunco party invitations out with the information on pretty cut-out hearts and invite everyone to make their favorite candy recipe to bring for everyone to enjoy. You could end up with one of the tastiest parties of all time. Don't forget to decorate with pink, white and red flowers in pretty little crystal vases on the table. Use little candy hearts in place of confetti and sprinkle on the table.

Candles make wonderful decorative pieces. You can give them away at the end of the night for several of your Bunco party gifts.

More Theme Party Ideas

A few more theme party ideas to help you out. Elaborate on these themes with festive invitations, playful decorations, thematic food and prizes. Have fun!

Snack/Appetizer Bunco Party

Have everyone bring their favorite munchie or create snack stations at each table with the many wonderful appetizer recipes included in this book.

Pasta Bunco Party

Serve different pasta sauces and noodles and create a fix-your-own pasta buffet.

Fall Harvest Theme Party

Decorate with fall colors and include pumpkins and gourds for decorations.

Western Theme Bunco Party

Cowgirl duds worn by all. "Cowboy Caviar" and "Western Meal-in-One" complement the theme, and don't forget the prize for best dressed.

Kid's Birthday Bunco Party

Limit the sets to two, instead of four.
Add snake eyes (rolling all ones and losing all your points).

Celebration of Color Theme

The hostess picks the color of the month and everyone dresses in it. The food coordinates with the color and the prizes do too.

New Year's Eve Couples Party

Allow everyone to bring a male guest for this special occasion.

Your Own Theme Party Ideas

Bunco Night
JOURNAL

Date of Party

_____

Hostess

_____

Party Theme

_____

Menu

_____

_____

_____

Winners

_____

_____

_____

_____

_____

Who Else Played

_____

_____

_____

**Memories
of the Evening**

_____

_____

_____

_____

_____

Bunco Night
JOURNAL

Date of Party

_____

Hostess

_____

Party Theme

_____

Menu

_____
_____
_____
_____

Winners

_____
_____
_____
_____
_____
_____

Who Else Played

_____
_____
_____

**Memories
of the Evening**

_____
_____
_____
_____
_____

Bunco Night
JOURNAL

Date of Party

_____

Hostess

_____

Party Theme

_____

Menu

_____

_____

_____

_____

Winners

_____

_____

_____

_____

_____

_____

Who Else Played

_____

_____

_____

_____

**Memories
of the Evening**

_____

_____

_____

_____

_____

_____

Bunco Night
JOURNAL

Date of Party

_____

Hostess

_____

Party Theme

_____

Menu

_____
_____
_____
_____

Winners

_____
_____
_____
_____
_____
_____

Who Else Played

_____
_____
_____

**Memories
of the Evening**

_____
_____
_____
_____
_____

Bunco Night
JOURNAL

Date of Party

_____

Hostess

_____

Party Theme

_____

Menu

_____
_____
_____
_____

Winners

_____
_____
_____
_____
_____
_____

Who Else Played

_____
_____
_____
_____

**Memories
of the Evening**

_____
_____
_____
_____
_____

Bunco Night
JOURNAL

Date of Party

_____

Hostess

_____

Party Theme

_____

Menu

_____
_____
_____
_____

Winners

_____
_____
_____
_____
_____
_____

Who Else Played

_____
_____
_____
_____

**Memories
of the Evening**

_____
_____
_____
_____
_____
_____

Bunco Night
JOURNAL

Date of Party

_____

Hostess

_____

Party Theme

_____

Menu

_____
_____
_____
_____

Winners

_____
_____
_____
_____
_____

Who Else Played

_____
_____
_____

**Memories
of the Evening**

_____
_____
_____
_____
_____

Bunco Night
JOURNAL

Date of Party

_____

Hostess

_____

Party Theme

_____

Menu

_____
_____
_____
_____

Winners

_____
_____
_____
_____
_____
_____

Who Else Played

_____
_____
_____
_____

**Memories
of the Evening**

_____
_____
_____
_____
_____
_____

Bunco Night
JOURNAL

Date of Party

_____

Hostess

_____

Party Theme

_____

Menu

_____
_____
_____
_____

Winners

_____
_____
_____
_____
_____

Who Else Played

_____
_____
_____

**Memories
of the Evening**

_____
_____
_____
_____
_____

Bunco Night
JOURNAL

Date of Party
_____

Hostess
_____

Party Theme
_____

Menu
_____
_____
_____
_____

Winners
_____
_____
_____
_____
_____

Who Else Played
_____
_____
_____
_____

Memories
of the Evening
_____
_____
_____
_____
_____
_____

Bunco Night
JOURNAL

Date of Party

_____

Hostess

_____

Party Theme

_____

Menu

_____
_____
_____
_____

Winners

_____
_____
_____
_____
_____

Who Else Played

_____
_____
_____
_____

**Memories
of the Evening**

_____
_____
_____
_____
_____

Bunco Night
JOURNAL

Date of Party

Hostess

Party Theme

Menu

Winners

Who Else Played

**Memories
of the Evening**

Bunco Night
JOURNAL

Date of Party

_____

Hostess

_____

Party Theme

_____

Menu

_____
_____
_____
_____

Winners

_____
_____
_____
_____
_____

Who Else Played

_____
_____
_____
_____

**Memories
of the Evening**

_____
_____
_____
_____
_____

Bunco Night
JOURNAL

Date of Party

_____

Hostess

_____

Party Theme

_____

Menu

_____
_____
_____
_____

Winners

_____
_____
_____
_____
_____
_____

Who Else Played

_____
_____
_____
_____

**Memories
of the Evening**

_____
_____
_____
_____
_____

Bunco Night
JOURNAL

Date of Party

_____

Hostess

_____

Party Theme

_____

Menu

_____
_____
_____
_____

Winners

_____
_____
_____
_____
_____

Who Else Played

_____
_____
_____

**Memories
of the Evening**

_____
_____
_____
_____
_____

Bunco Night
JOURNAL

Date of Party

_____

Hostess

_____

Party Theme

_____

Menu

_____
_____
_____
_____

Winners

_____
_____
_____
_____
_____

Who Else Played

_____
_____
_____

**Memories
of the Evening**

_____
_____
_____
_____
_____

Bunco Night
JOURNAL

Date of Party

_____

Hostess

_____

Party Theme

_____

Menu

_____
_____
_____
_____

Winners

_____
_____
_____
_____
_____
_____

Who Else Played

_____
_____
_____

**Memories
of the Evening**

_____
_____
_____
_____
_____

Bunco Night
JOURNAL

Date of Party

_____

Hostess

_____

Party Theme

_____

Menu

_____
_____
_____
_____

Winners

_____
_____
_____
_____
_____
_____

Who Else Played

_____
_____
_____

**Memories
of the Evening**

_____
_____
_____
_____
_____
_____

Bunco Night
JOURNAL

Date of Party

_____

Hostess

_____

Party Theme

_____

Menu

_____
_____
_____
_____

Winners

_____
_____
_____
_____
_____

Who Else Played

_____
_____
_____

**Memories
of the Evening**

_____
_____
_____
_____

Bunco Night
JOURNAL

Date of Party

_____

Hostess

_____

Party Theme

_____

Menu

_____
_____
_____
_____

Winners

_____
_____
_____
_____
_____

Who Else Played

_____
_____
_____

**Memories
of the Evening**

_____
_____
_____
_____
_____

Bunco Night
JOURNAL

Date of Party

_____

Hostess

_____

Party Theme

_____

Menu

_____
_____
_____

Winners

_____
_____
_____
_____
_____

Who Else Played

_____
_____
_____

**Memories
of the Evening**

_____
_____
_____
_____
_____

Bunco Night
JOURNAL

Date of Party

_____

Hostess

_____

Party Theme

_____

Menu

_____
_____
_____

Winners

_____
_____
_____
_____
_____

Who Else Played

_____
_____
_____

**Memories
of the Evening**

_____
_____
_____
_____
_____

Bunco Night
JOURNAL

Date of Party

_____

Hostess

_____

Party Theme

_____

Menu

_____
_____
_____
_____

Winners

_____
_____
_____
_____
_____

Who Else Played

_____
_____
_____

**Memories
of the Evening**

_____
_____
_____
_____
_____

Bunco Night
JOURNAL

Date of Party

_____

Hostess

_____

Party Theme

_____

Menu

_____
_____
_____
_____

Winners

_____
_____
_____
_____
_____

Who Else Played

_____
_____
_____

**Memories
of the Evening**

_____
_____
_____
_____
_____

Bunco Night
JOURNAL

Date of Party

_____

Hostess

_____

Party Theme

_____

Menu

_____
_____
_____
_____

Winners

_____
_____
_____
_____
_____

Who Else Played

_____
_____
_____

**Memories
of the Evening**

_____
_____
_____
_____
_____

Bunco Night
JOURNAL

Date of Party

_____

Hostess

_____

Party Theme

_____

Menu

_____

_____

_____

_____

Winners

_____

_____

_____

_____

_____

Who Else Played

_____

_____

_____

**Memories
of the Evening**

_____

_____

_____

_____

_____

Bunco Night
JOURNAL

Date of Party

Hostess

Party Theme

Menu

Winners

Who Else Played

**Memories
of the Evening**